MAKING a DIFFERENCE

Commandments and Community

MAKING a DIFFERENCE

Commandments and Community

by

Michal Shekel

KTAV Publishing House, Inc., Hoboken, NJ

Contents

אַהֲבַת צִיּוֹן

בַּל תַּשְׁחִית

בִּקּוּר חוֹלִים

צַעַר בַּעֲלֵי חַיִּים

גְּמִילוּת חֲסָדִים

חֶסֶד שֶׁל אֱמֶת

לְשׁוֹן הָרָע

כָּל יִשְׂרָאֵל עֲרֵבִים זֶה לָזֶה

שְׁלוֹם בַּיִת

תַּלְמוּד תּוֹרָה

צְדָקָה

פִּקּוּחַ נֶפֶשׁ

פִּדְיוֹן שְׁבוּיִים

מָעוֹת חִטִּים

הִדּוּר פְּנֵי זָקֵן

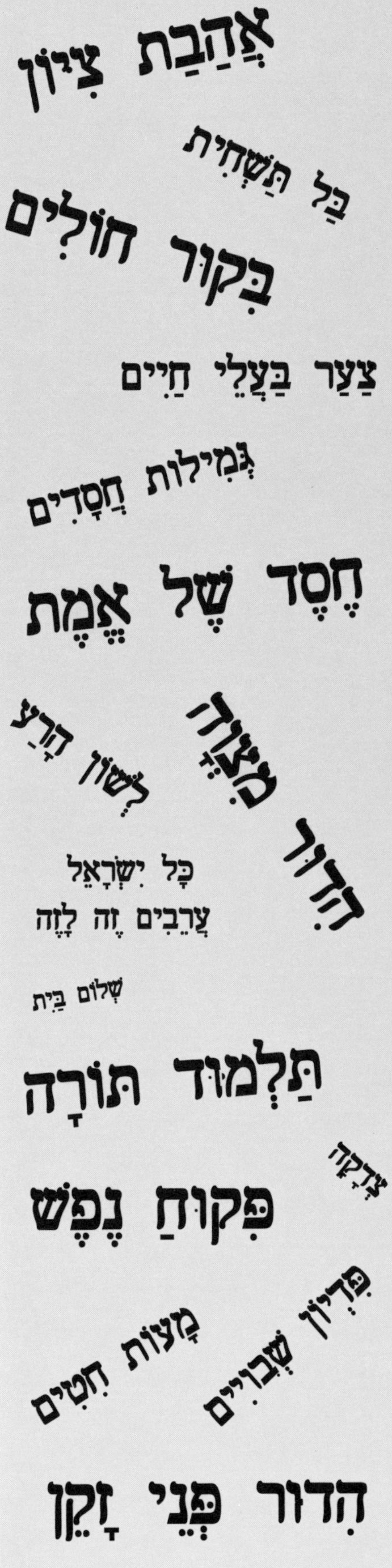

for

Ethan

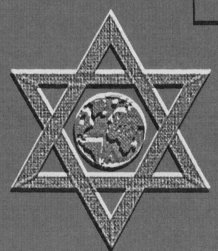

The Union of American
Hebrew Congregations

KEREN

· 5

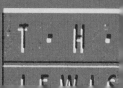

מִצְוֹת
positive commandments

תַּרְיַ"ג מִצְוֹת
613 mitzvot

According to the Talmud, there are 613 mitzvot in the Torah. The Hebrew letters whose numerical value equals 613 spell out the word *Taryag*, so we call these the *Taryag mitzvot*.

There are 248 yes-do mitzvot. These are mitzvot that God wants us to do, such as praying and honoring our parents. In Hebrew these are called *mitzvot aseh*. There are 365 that are the don't-do kind. These are called *mitzvot lo taaseh*. Don't steal and don't kill are just two examples.

248 + 365 = 613

Introduction

What do surgery, travel, and painting with watercolors have in common? In one way or another, they all fulfill mitzvot, positive acts or deeds that are part of a Jewish lifestyle. The word mitzvah literally means "commandment." When we perform a mitzvah we are fulfilling our obligation to God. Mitzvot are the way in which we show what we believe as Jews.

You Don't Have to Be Jewish

Actually, according to Jewish belief, everybody, Jewish or not, has God-given responsibilities. In Judaism, the commandments given to all humanity are called the seven *Noahide* laws. The word Noahide comes from the biblical Noah, who is considered to have been the ancestor of the entire human race, as well as a role model for being a good, moral person.

The seven Noahide commandments are:

1. Not to deny God's existence.
2. Not to speak badly of God.
3. Not to murder.
4. Not to take part in forbidden physical relationships.
5. Not to steal.
6. Not to eat a limb that is torn off a living animal.
7. To establish courts in order to make sure that the other six laws are obeyed by everyone.

613 and Counting . . .

Tradition tells us that there are 613 mitzvot in the Torah. Other mitzvot have been added to the 613 based on interpretations over the centuries. The mitzvot fall into two categories. There are commandments which are considered obligations of Jews towards God, called in Hebrew *mitzvot bein adam la-makom.* There are also commandments defining the relationship between human beings. In Hebrew these are known as *mitzvot bein adam le-havero.* Many of the commandments between God and humanity deal with rituals. These include instructions for celebrating Shabbat and holy days. Some of these commandments are no longer practiced; for example, animal sacrifice, which was a major part of ritual in ancient Israel.

מִצְוֹת בֵּין אָדָם לַמָּקוֹם
relationship between
man and God

מִצְוֹת בֵּין אָדָם לְחַבֵרוֹ
relationship between
humans

The number 613 is symbolic, teaching us that there are so many ways in which we can put our Jewish beliefs into practice. It is symbolic in that 248 represents the limbs of the body, and 365 the days of the year, meaning that we should devote all our abilities and all days of the year to mitzvot. This can be done in ways we often don't think of as being commandments, such as visiting someone. or adopting a pet at an animal shelter. Mitzvot are more than good deeds, they are requirements. We must do them whether we want to or not. This is part of our covenant, our "holy contract," with God.

Mitzvot provide us with spiritual road signs, leading us closer to God and the divine aspect within us which we call *tzelem elohim,* God's image. In Jewish tradition we believe that all human beings have the potential to do wonderful things and to commit terrible acts. In Hebrew our inner potentials are called *yetzer ha-tov,* the good inclination, or *yetzer ha-ra,* the evil inclination. We hope that by performing mitzvot our good tendencies will overcome our evil inclination. Then we will be strengthened spiritually, moving ever closer to God and fulfilling God's desire for human potential.

צֶלֶם אֱלֹהִים
God's image

יֵצֶר הַטּוֹב
positive inclination

The Siddur, our Jewish prayerbook, reminds us of the importance of doing mitzvot. It uses this lesson from the Talmud to teach us about the two types of mitzvot, those between humanity and God, and those between human beings:

יֵצֶר הָרַע
evil inclination

These are the things that are timeless, so that one enjoys their results in this world and in the world-to-come: honoring father and mother, performing deeds of lovingkindness, attending the house of study morning and evening, welcoming the stranger, visiting the sick, welcoming bride and groom, accompanying the dead to the cemetery, praying sincerely, making peace among people. The study of Torah is equal to them all because it leads to them all.

Keeping Track of Mitzvot

While it is hard to pinpoint all 613 commandments, there have been many efforts to help Jews "do the right thing." When these efforts are put in writing, they are known as codes of law, or just codes for short. At various times in Jewish history, rabbis familiar with the mitzvot wrote codes to help people keep track of what they should do. One of the earliest was written by a twelfth-century Spanish rabbi, Moses Maimonides, known as Rambam in Hebrew. Rambam called his work the *Mishneh Torah,* the "Repetition of the Torah." The most famous code is the *Shulchan Aruch,* the "Set Table," written by a sixteenth-century rabbi, Joseph Caro. These codes arranged the mitzvot by categories and could be used for reference, hence their popularity. They cover everything from prayer to hygiene to work to issues of life and death.

The underlying idea of the mitzvot between human beings is that we are all connected to each other. An individual mitzvah, such as not gossiping, affects the whole community. A communal mitzvah, such as caring for the sick, helps the individual. Over the years, various groups have arisen to fulfill particular mitzvot. Some of these groups still exist, others have disappeared and been replaced by newer groups. The purpose of each group is to fill a need in the community. You may have heard of some of these groups, but probably didn't know that they were established to fulfill a mitzvah. You probably know people who belong to one or more Jewish organizations. They do so in order to fulfill mitzvot, for a sense of Jewish pride, and for the welfare of the entire community.

In the rest of this book you will look at many different mitzvot. You may be surprised how many activities are considered mitzvot. You have probably performed a number of mitzvot without even knowing it. You will understand that

מִשְׁנֵה תּוֹרָה
"Repetition of the Torah"

שֻׁלְחָן עָרוּךְ
"Set Table"

In the sixteenth century, Safed became the major Jewish community in Eretz Yisrael. One of its most famous residents was Rabbi Joseph Caro, author of the *Shulchan Aruch.* This book soon spread throughout the Jewish world, and contains the rules for leading a religious Jewish life. Shown here is the title page from the first edition, printed in Venice in 1655.

mitzvot are deeds that show our love of God, pride in Judaism, and concern for humanity and the world.

Why Should We Do the Right Thing?

While the codes tell us what to do, there is another body of literature that tells us why. This is known as musar, ethical literature. Musar provides the spiritual reasons for doing the right thing. Musar tries to give purpose to life, to our relationships with God and each other. While the ideas in musar bring us closer to God, the way in which they do this is very down to earth.

> It is good and right that in every city there be a group of qualified [enlightened] volunteers who are prepared and ready at all times for any situation where a Jewish man or woman must be rescued from distress. We are obligated to exert ourselves on behalf of our neighbor's ox or sheep that is lost, to keep it until our neighbor asks for it; how much more so with respect to the owner! As it is written: "The poor who are outcasts you shall bring to the house" (Isaiah 58:7.)
>
> —Sha'arei Teshuvah (Gates of Repentance), Third Gate 71

Some mitzvot are very easy to fulfill, others can be quite difficult. Yet performing mitzvot is a prime Jewish responsibility. In doing mitzvot, and accepting these responsibilities, whether as individuals or through groups, you are fulfilling the precept "do not separate yourself from the community."

מוּסָר
ethics

Rabbi Israel Salanter of Lithuania developed a special musar yeshiva dedicated to the study of ethical literature. A daily session was set aside for special musar instruction. The leaders of the musar movement also established yeshivot at Khelm, Slobodka, and Novaredok.

Teachings from Tradition

A person should always provoke the good inclination against the evil inclination.

<Berachot 5a>

I created the evil inclination and I created the Torah as the antidote.

<Kiddushin 30b>

The evil inclination, behaves like a guest at first and then becomes the master.

<Beresheet Rabbah 22:6>

One who observes mitzvot
preserves one's own life

שׁוֹמֵר מִצְוָה
שׁוֹמֵר נַפְשׁוֹ

<Pirke Avot 4:12>

צְדָקָה

Tzedakah:
Charity and Justice

How do you decide how much your baseball cards are worth? Do they mean a lot to you because you like the players? Do you have a card that few other kids have, and so they want to trade for it? Do you go to a store and ask how much you can sell it for? If these are tough questions, think of how much more difficult it would be if we all had to decide the value of everything: food, clothing, housing, entertainment!

These are issues people had to consider before the invention of money. Before coins were invented, people bartered and traded. The problem with bartering is that when you find something you want, you have to offer something else of equivalent value in exchange. It may be difficult to estimate the respective values of two totally different items. Even if the values are judged correctly, you're out of luck if the other person doesn't like what you are offering. With money came standardization. The value of things could be fixed.

Coins revolutionized the world. They made it possible to work for a wage. This in turn created new jobs. Coins also brought problems. With the creation of new jobs, fewer and fewer people farmed. If you were a farmer and couldn't sell your produce, you would lack money but would still have food to eat. If you weren't a farmer and had no job, and no coins, you had no food.

מַטְבֵּעַ/מַטְבְּעוֹת
coins/coin

Ancient Hebrew coins from the Hasmonean and Bar Kochba periods

Polish coins with Hebrew inscriptions

שֶׁקֶל
shekel

צְדָקָה
justice, righteousness

How could you survive? In the Jewish community, one answer comes from the mitzvot we perform.

Where Does Money Come From?

Coins first arrived on the scene in the seventh century B.C.E. in a number of places. Some were shaped like beans and made out of metal. They were stamped with a lion insignia, representing the king of Lydia in western Turkey. On the other side they had a mark attesting that they were real. At about the same time small, flat pieces of silver that were stamped with an official emblem were used for money in India. Paper money was invented by the Chinese around 800 C.E. There was one inconvenient aspect. The wind could blow it away, and so it was dubbed "flying money" by the Chinese.

Coins turned out to be very convenient. It's easier to go shopping with a pocketful of coins than with a bag of wampum shells, a wagonload of farm produce, or a herd of cattle. The precious metals make it desirable for people to sell things. Abraham was able to acquire the cave of Machpelah as a burial place for Sarah by paying 400 silver shekels, a shekel being a unit of weight. Today, the shekel is a both a coin and a paper bill; it is the official currency of Israel.

If you had been a Jew living in twelfth-century Poland, and had been fortunate enough to have a coin, you would have been able to read what was inscribed on it. Polish coins had Hebrew lettering on them. These letters spelled out the name of the mintmaster, the person in charge of making the coins. There are Polish coins with the Hebrew names Abraham, Jacob, and Menahem. Because Jews were mintmasters in many parts of Europe, Hebrew lettering often appears on medieval coins. This only began to change in the late Middle Ages, when this occupation was closed to Jews, along with many other crafts and positions.

The Mitzvah of Tzedakah

If you were to ask someone to describe a mitzvah, chances are they would tell you about giving tzedakah. While the Hebrew word tzedakah means "justice" or "righteousness," it has a more popular meaning as well, giving money to charity. People give tzedakah on various occasions: for the birth of a child, a wedding or birthday, a graduation. People give tzedakah to remember someone who has died. When you become a Bar or Bat Mitzvah, one of your first responsibilities as a Jewish adult may be to decide where to donate a portion of the gift money you have received.

There are different ways of giving tzedakah. You can do it openly so that everyone knows what you're doing, or you can do it quietly, so that only you are aware of it. Which way of giving do you think is a greater mitzvah?

Making the Top Ten List

Moses Maimonides, a twelfth-century rabbi born in Spain, had his own opinion on this subject. He said that there were eight levels of tzedakah. This is how he ranked them from highest to lowest:

1. Giving a gift, loan, business partnership, or job that enables the recipient to be self-supporting, making other charity unnecessary.
2. Giving where neither giver nor recipient knows the other's identity; for example, by putting money in a tzedakah box.
3. Giving where the giver doesn't know the recipient, but the recipient knows who gave the money.
4. Where the recipient doesn't know the giver, but the giver knows who got the money.
5. Giving before being asked to give.
6. Giving when asked to give.
7. Giving less than one should, but being nice about it.
8. Giving, but not being nice about it.

Several other Jewish scholars drew up lists of levels of tzedakah, though no one came up with a top ten list. Moses of Coucy, who lived in thirteenth-century France, had a top nine list. He said that the highest form of tzedakah occurs when the giver and recipient do not know each other, while the lowest is to give grudgingly.

An interesting perspective is provided by the fourteenth-century Spanish poet Israel ben Joseph al-Nakawa, who had a top five list. He agreed with Maimonides that the highest level of giving is to help a person become self-sufficient. Al-Nakawa also dealt with another aspect of tzedakah: who should receive it? Here is al-Nakawa's top nine list, from lowest to highest:

רִי מֹשֶׁה בֶּן מֵימָן
רַמְבַּם

The autograph of Maimonides

A silver tzedakah box, Germany 1880

Nathan Straus started the Straus Milk Fund, which distributed pasteurized milk from his own laboratory to the poor. He charged much less than the daries did. After 20 years he was able to close his pasteurization plants, for by then, New York as well as other states had passed laws that required pasteurization and inspection of milk.

נַדְבָן

philanthropist

Leslie H. Wexner
Mr Wexner is the founder of "The Limited", a clothing chain with over 3,000 national and international stores.

1. Giving some money to a beggar who goes door to door.
2. Giving shelter to people passing through town.
3. Providing a dowry for a poor bride.
4. Providing poor grooms with household items.
5. Helping a poor but decent person.
6. Helping a poor person who has seen better days to live according to his or her prior standard of living.
7. Giving a loan to someone who is sensitive about accepting charity.
8. Providing a needy scholar with a loan or grant in a respect ful manner.
9. Giving to the poor of the community according to their individual needs and without shaming them.

The Big Givers

Some people are fortunate enough to have a great deal of wealth. Those who use their wealth for the good of the entire community are called philanthropists. One such person was Nathan Straus (1848–1931). He created a successful department store chain called Abraham and Straus. Other people were not as fortunate as he was. In the early part of the twentieth century, he used his money to help some of them. When people were unemployed he provided food, shelter, and coal. Interestingly, he did not give these things away. He charged a penny for food and a nickel for a basket of coal. Which of Maimonides' eight rungs of tzedakah was he following?

Other philanthropists set up funds that give money to various causes. The money may be used to send children to school or to feed people. Some philanthropists have special interests, such as Israel, the Holocaust, or new immigrants.

Murray Lender, of Lender's Bagels, devotes both time and money to the United Jewish Appeal, which funds Jewish communal programs in the United States and Israel. Part of being involved in such an organization is encouraging other fortunate individuals to use their wealth for the good of the community. The best way to do this is by setting an example and challenging others to follow it.

The Wexner Foundation, for example, trains future American Jewish leaders. This family foundation sponsors special educational programs around the country for people targeted as having leadership potential. The foundation also provides scholarship money for rabbinical students and graduate students in Jewish studies.

Film director Steven Spielberg has donated to Brandeis University and other institutions of learning. He also has taken a personal interest in making sure that the Holocaust is not forgotten. He has set up an organization to contact Holocaust survivors and record their stories.

Both individuals and entire families may engage in philanthropic activities. In many cases, an organization is set up to distribute the philanthropist's tzedakah. This organization, called a foundation, may have a specific goal. Sometimes it gives money to other organizations that distribute the funds where needed. Sometimes individuals can apply directly, as with college scholarships. In some cases, funding is set aside only for programs that the philanthropist regards as important. Which rungs of Rambam's ladder are covered by philanthropists? Which follow al-Nakawa's guidelines?

When the Well Runs Dry

A serious problem is being faced by many countries that provide tzedakah to the needy through tax money. What do you do when there is a great need and you run out of money? Some governments are turning to local communities and religious organizations for help. These groups depend on private individuals and tzedakah that is voluntarily contributed. How do you decide who shall receive tzedakah if there is only a limited amount of money available?

Here is a real problem faced by many towns around the country. People continue to donate money, but not as much as in years past, because they are not earning enough. Many people in the community are part of the working poor: earning so little that they must decide between spending money to pay their rent or taking a peanut butter sandwich to work. Winter is coming. Your tzedakah organization knows that both food and shelter are going to be very important in the coming winter, but you don't have enough money to supply both needs for all the poor of your community. What do you do? Would creating a list of priorities, like al-Nakawa's list, be helpful? How do you provide tzedakah, not only charity, but justice and righteousness to the needy people in your community?

Mr. and Mrs Steven Spielberg at a Weizmann Institute of Science event. Steven Spielberg is a movie director and producer. His films include *Schindler's List* and *Star Wars*. His wife, Kate Capshaw, is a well-known movie actress.

Jacob Schiff
Schiff was an outstanding patron of learning, giving funds to institutions of learning ranging from Harvard and Barnard to the Jewish Theological Seminary and the Haifa Technion.

Teachings from Tradtion

Do not harden your heart and shut your hand against a needy kinsman.

<Devarim 15:7>

The one who gives tzedakah secretly is greater than Moses.

<Bava Batra 9b>

Charity outweighs

all other mitzvot.

שְׁקוּלָה צְדָקָה

כְּנֶגֶד כָּל הַמִּצְוֹות

<Bava Batra 9a>

כָּל יִשְׂרָאֵל עֲרֵבִים זֶה לָזֶה

Kol Yisrael Arevim Zeh la-Zeh:
We are responsible for each other

What do you want to be when you grow up? You've probably heard that question so often that you are sick and tired of it. Oddly enough, it is a very modern question. Even a century ago you might not have had a choice. You would have gone into the family business or into one of the limited number of occupations permitted to Jews.

Historically, there is a stereotype as to the types of work Jews did. Knights, farmers, and explorers are not images that come to mind as Jewish occupations. Yet there were Jews involved in these and other activities—when permitted. Most frequently, Jews were pushed into doing work of benefit to the ruler. Those who could not fulfill that role held marginal positions.

In nineteenth-century Eastern Europe, many Jews made a meager living as peddlers, an occupation brought to the United States when they came here to find fortune in the "golden land." In medieval Europe, Jews were forced into the business of moneylending. In Moslem Spain, Jews had a greater choice of activities, including trade and medicine.

Because of the stereotypes and the historical restrictions, we forget that some Jews had interesting professions. Jews were among the leaders in map-making and designing navigational equipment during the age of exploration. Among the

A Jewish peddler in pre-Holocaust Poland.

Jewish peddlers on the Lower East Side, New York City, 1900

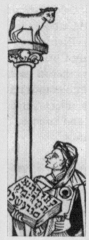

Anti-Semitic picture of Yosel of Rosheim, the "Court Jew" of Emperor Charles V. In one hand is the Hebrew Bible and in the other a bag of money.

כָּל יִשְׂרָאֵל
עֲרֵבִים זֶה לָזֶה

Jews are responsible for each other.

שְׁתַּדְלָן

Jewish diplomat

David Sarnoff (1891-1971) who began as a messenger boy and wireless operator. He rose to become head of RCA. Mr Sarnoff was politically active on behalf of many Jewish causes.

explorers who benefited from their labors were Christopher Columbus and Vasco da Gama. Jews, including many women, were among the early printers in Italy. Until the rise of medieval guilds, Jews were involved in all types of crafts. In Navarre, Spain, there are even records of Jewish jugglers and lion tamers!

Eventually, Jews were forced into certain professions, specifically those that were of benefit to the ruler. Even under these circumstances, Jews still had a measure of independence. Within the Jewish community there were many governing positions, many of them strictly voluntary: running organizations, heading the synagogue, making sure everyone was fed and clothed, even making sure that every couple had a suitable wedding. The underlying idea was the concern of the community for its own members.

The Mitzvah of *Kol Yisrael Arevim Zeh la-Zeh*

During the best and worst of times, Jewish communal organizations did the best they could to see to it that minimal standards of communal needs were met. The goal was to fulfill the mitzvah of *kol yisrael arevim zeh la-zeh,* "all Jews are responsible for each other." Over the centuries, Jewish communities have developed many ways of performing this mitzvah. Some are still in use today; others have died out due to changes in lifestyle and historical circumstances. As new needs arise, new responses are developed.

As in any group, some people are in a better position to help than others. In past centuries, even when Jewish life was strictly regulated and opportunities for Jews restricted, certain outstanding individuals attained positions outside the Jewish community and were able to use their special status to fulfill the mitzvah of *kol yisrael arevim zeh la-zeh.* These individuals are generally called shtadlanim, a Yiddish word derived from the Hebrew root meaning "to make an effort."

Shtadlanim had to have tremendous diplomatic skills. They were the go-betweens on behalf of the Jewish community, dealing with the officials of the host country. Shtadlanim came in contact with the rich and famous of the nations in which Jews lived. A shtadlan would ask the king for protection so that anti-Semitic mobs would not harm the Jewish community. In the fourteenth century, shtadlanim asked for the pope's help in keeping the Inquisition away from the Jewish community.

Friends in High Places

Shtadlanim gained access to the powerful because of the services they could provide to the government. They would help any ruler who allowed Jews to settle in his territory. Because they were so often at the royal court, the shtadlanim are often called "court Jews." Court Jews arranged loans for rulers who had a "cash flow" problem. They made sure that the ruler's army was paid and supplied. Because Jews were usually multilingual, they often acted as interpreters and translators.

In the best of times, the court Jews could use their contacts with the ruler to aid their people. The ruler would provide protection from rioters and prevent expulsions. In the worst of times, the court Jews were among the first victims. If a ruler did not want to repay his loans, he simply expelled the Jewish community from his territory. A court Jew could be imprisoned, expelled, or killed.

The most famous court Jew was Joseph Suss Oppenheimer, who was finance minister to the duke of Wurttemberg in the eighteenth century. When the duke died, Oppenheimer's enemies at court had him imprisoned. He was told he could save his life if he converted to Christianity. Oppenheimer refused to do this, saying he would not convert even if he was made emperor. Because of his refusal, he was executed.

In modern times, Jews have also held high offices. Many, such as Senator Arlen Spector of Pennsylvania, are elected to Congress. Others have been appointed to important posts, including the Supreme Court and the president's cabinet.. Henry Kissinger was secretary of state for President Richard Nixon. Kissinger performed many important tasks, such as helping end the war in Vietnam and renewing relations with China. Mickey Kantor was commerce secretary for President Bill Clinton. Among his assignments was making sure that American companies were given opportunities to do business in China and Japan.

Shtadlanim and court Jews were not always well-liked in the Jewish community. Some felt that they had "sold out" to the secular world, others resented the community's depen-

Edgar Miles Bronfman
Bronfman is the chairman and chief executive officer of the multinational firm of the Seagram Company Ltd. In addition he is a dynamic communal leader and philanthropist who uses his influence and skills for the benefit of the Jewish community. Most important, is his position as president of the World Jewish Congress. Bronfman and the WJC have been actively fighting the Swiss government to recover the hidden assets of Jewish Holocaust victims.
In addition, Mr. Bronfman is Chairman of the ADL, UJA, American Society for Technion and a member of the Council on Foreign Relations.

Joseph Suss Oppenheim

Secretary of State Henry Kissinger (*right*) talks to Abba Eban and Yigal Allon during his shuttle diplomacy which led to a settlement between Israel and Egypt in 1979.

dence on the court Jews for survival. Whatever their motives, these Jews with ties to the outside world enabled many communities to carry out the mitzvah of *kol yisrael arevim zeh la-zeh.*

Some Advice on Dealing with Power

Jewish writings since ancient times have displayed mixed feelings about involvements with government and those who hold secular power.

Pirke Avot is a section of the Mishnah, set down in about 200 C.E. Here is a centuries-old comment from it about dealing with political leaders. Do you think it is true?

> Be very cautious in dealing with the authorities, for they will not allow you near them unless it is for their own purposes. They act friendly when it benefits them, but do not stand by you in your time of need.
>
> —Pirke Avot 2:3

But a word of warning appears in the very next paragraph. How does this apply to shtadlanim and their critics?

> Hillel says: Do not separate yourself from the community, do not believe [solely] in yourself until the day of your death, and do not judge another until you have been in his place.
>
> —Pirke Avot 2:4

Two more pieces of advice can also be found in the Talmud:

> "[Wrongdoers] who have spread their terror in the land of the living." Rabbi Hisda said: This refers to a communal leader who makes himself unduly feared by the community for other than religious reasons.
>
> —Rosh Hashanah 17a

> When the community is in trouble, do not say, "I will go home and eat and drink, and all will be well with me." . . . Rather, involve yourself in the community's distress, as was demonstrated by Moses (Exodus 27:12). In this way Moses said, "Since Israel is in trouble, I will share their burden." Anyone who shares a community's distress will be rewarded and will witness the community's consolation.
>
> —Ta'anit 11a

פִּרְקֵי אָבוֹת
Sayings of the Fathers

Which of these comments can be applied to political leaders? Which can be applied to Jewish leaders? Which apply to all of us? Do you think that Jewish tradition considers it a mitzvah to take part in government and communal affairs?

Ask Not What Your Country Can Do for You

The American Jewish community has created many organizations to provide help for Jews around the world. These groups serve all Jews regardless of background or beliefs. They are supported by the majority of the Jewish community.

The leading Jewish communal organization is the Jewish federation. Jewish federations can be found in almost every Jewish community in the United States. The federations raise money for the services provided within the American Jewish community: schools, nursing homes, vocational services, counseling services, and community relations.

The fundraising campaign is called the United Jewish Appeal (UJA). UJA began in 1938, in response to Kristallnacht, the first step in Nazi Germany's campaign of destruction. With the creation of the State of Israel, most UJA money went to help that nation develop. Eventually, the United Jewish Appeal combined its fundraising efforts with the Jewish federations. Their combined campaign truly shows how all Jews are responsible for each other. The funds raised in this country go to help Jews everywhere: in Israel, the former Soviet Union, and wherever Jewish communities face emergencies.

Aside from fundraising, UJA and federation provide another important service. Through a variety of programs, they train volunteers to be leaders of the Jewish community, so that future generations can fulfill the mitzvah of *kol yisrael arevim zeh la-zeh*.

Ask What You Can Do for Your Country

There are other important Jewish organizations that have arisen to fulfill the mitzvah of helping all people. One is the Anti-Defamation League of B'nai B'rith (ADL). Originally, the ADL was founded to fight anti-Semitism in the United States. Today its mission is to fight racism as well. Another group that has expanded its mission from fighting anti-

Israeli stamp honoring the UJA

United Jewish Appeal UJA

Anti-Defamation League ADL

American Jewish Committee AJC

The ADL was founded in 1913 "to end the defamation of the Jewish people . . . and to secure justice and fair treatment for all people alike." It is one of the nation's oldest and leading Jewish human relations agencies.

Henry Jones, a founder of B'nai B'rith, largest of Jewish fraternal orders, in 1843, from a drawing by George D. M. Peixotto

Dr. Chaim Weizmann

הַכְנָסַת אוֹרְחִים
hospitality

Semitism is the American Jewish Committee. Today it tries to build up Christian-Jewish understanding. The American Jewish Congress focuses on political and constitutional issues in its fight to maintain civil liberties for all Americans.

Anyone Can Grow Up to Be President
The most important thing to keep in mind about the responsibilities of Jews toward one another and toward the rest of humanity is that anyone can fulfill these mitzvot. You can do so in small ways by respecting others, you can do it in larger ways by taking part in the political process. What we can learn from the court Jews and shtadlanim is that no matter what your occupation, you too can be called on to help.

Take the case of a Russian-born chemist who, in 1910, became director of a laboratory for the British navy. Because of his crucial work during World War I, he was able to help the Jewish community. The chemist helped get the British government to issue the Balfour Declaration in 1917, endorsing the establishment of a Jewish national home in Palestine. When the State of Israel was born in 1948, Chaim Weizmann became its first president, yet again serving the Jewish community and fulfilling the mitzvah of *kol yisrael arevim zeh la-zeh*.

Hospitality
Jewish responsibility for each other extends to *hakhnasat orhim*, hospitality. The Midrash tells the story of Abraham and Sarah, who built a tent with four entrances, so that travellers coming from any direction could find immediate hospitality. In olden days, when travel was slow and dangerous, synagogues felt responsible for Jewish travellers, and arranged for food and lodging with members of their congregation. European synagogues even set aside special rooms where travellers could eat and slieep.

Today, some synagogues have special hospitality committees, who will make arrangements to house and to feed visitors, students, and military personel who wish to spend Shabbat or the holidays with a Jewish family.

Teachings from Tradition

You shall be holy, for I Adonai your God am Holy.

<Vayikra 19:2>

As God is called compassionate and and merciful, you too must be compassionate and merciful, giving freely of yourself.

<Sifre, Devarim 46>

Woe to the one who says: "peace be unto me," and does not join the community in its time of need.

<Shevet Musar, Eliyahu HaCohen>

If you do not	אִם אֵין אַתָּה
pity your friend	מְרַחֵם עַל חֲבֵרְךָ
nobody	אֵין לְךָ
will pity you.	מְרַחֵם

<Tanhuma>

פִּקוּחַ נֶפֶשׁ

Pikuah Nefesh: Saving a Life

We tend to view our civilization as very advanced, especially in terms of science and technology. That is why it is surprising to find out that in ancient times people had skills we consider very modern. Chief among these skills was the practice of medicine.

When we think of ancient medicine it is usually associated with superstition and incantations. Yet even thousands of years ago true medicine was practiced. Trepanation, a type of brain surgery, dates back to ancient Egypt and is mentioned in the Talmud as well (Ohalot 2:3). In India, plastic surgery was highly developed. Both in ancient Israel and in the Diaspora, Jews practiced medicine.

In biblical times, public health was a major concern. This is illustrated by the many mitzvot discussing illnesses, skin diseases, and sores mentioned in the Torah. The examinations were done by the priests, and some of the measures used were quarantine and hygiene.

In postbiblical times, a more familiar type of medicine was practiced. The Talmud speaks of both doctors and surgeons. Doctors dispensed medicinal herbs and balms. Surgeons performed amputations, cesarean deliveries, and even cut away at wounds to help with proper healing. In the Talmud there is mention of a *bet shayish*, a house or room with marble walls,

בֵּית שַׁיִשׁ
room with marble walls

that was used for surgery. There is even mention of a special apron worn by the surgeon while at work. The Talmud also advises people not to live in towns where there was no medical service available. According to the Jerusalem Talmud, it is *forbidden* to live in a town where there is no physician (Kiddushin 4:12, 66b).

In medieval times, Jews served on the faculty of the medical college in Salerno, Italy. The great Moses Maimonides, called Rambam in Hebrew, was a doctor as well as a rabbi. His patients included the sultan of Egypt and his family. Rambam composed an oath setting forth the responsibilities and duties of the physician. Some doctors, upon graduating from medical school, recite the Maimonidean oath instead of the Hippocratic oath which has long been traditional in secular medical schools. Both call for the physician to treat the patient to the best of the doctor's abilities, regardless of all other concerns.

An Oath or a Prayer?

An oath is a vow or a promise. What Maimonides wrote is actually a prayer to be recited by the physician in the morning. In it he asks God to make his mind clear and enlightened, thinking only of the patient he is attending. He prays that everything he has learned about science and medicine will be in his mind.

> Keep far from me the delusion that I can accomplish everything. Give me the strength, the will, and the chance to increase my knowledge. Today, I have knowledge to do things that I could not have imagined yesterday, for the art is great, but the human mind presses on tirelessly.

Rambam then asks for help in focusing on the patient and requests that God help him in this task, "for without Your help one cannot succeed in even the smallest of things."

In this prayer, Maimonides is conscious of the physician's great responsibility, but also acknowledges that the physician is a human being with human limitations. Despite these limitations, conscientious doctors will work to the best of their ability to save human lives.

Medicine is often considered a Jewish profession. Thus it is surprising to learn that in modern times, Jews often met obstacles when it came to the practice of medicine. Quotas

שְׁבוּעָה
oath, promise

Michael Reese Hospital in Chicago named after the Jewish philanthropist (1817–1878). It was built by the United Hebrew Charities. The hospital is still in existence.

The Touro Infirmary, endowed by Judah Touro in New Orleans. He gave continuously for health services during his life, as well as for religious, cultural, and patriotic causes, and to help the poor.

Organized to fight anti-Semitism, the Anti-Defamation League commemorated its seventieth anniversary with this poster, presented here by Theodore Freedman (*on the left*), director of the National Intergroup Relations division, and Larry J. Sachnowitz, president of the Gulf State Advertising Agency of Houston, Texas.

פְּקוּחַ נֶפֶשׁ

saving a life

existed in American medical schools beginning in the 1920s. They were meant to keep Jews out of the programs. Further difficulties were met when hospitals refused to hire Jewish doctors. This is one reason there are so many Jewish hospitals in major cities. They arose out of a need to train Jewish doctors refused admittance at American medical schools and teaching hospitals.

One reason so many Jews are drawn to the practice of medicine, is that medical care fulfills one of the highest mitzvot—that of saving human life.

Jews Need Not Apply

Jews have responded to acts of bias in many ways over the years. One way is to provide in the Jewish community what is denied by the greater community. The Albert Einstein College of Medicine at Yeshiva University was an early response to Jewish quotas in medical schools. Fortunately, such quotas are now illegal. The Einstein College of Medicine today provides fine medical training to students of all backgrounds.

Many Jewish organizations have dealt specifically with issues of prejudice. The Anti-Defamation League of B'nai B'rith keeps track of hate groups. It also provides curricula on tolerance that are used in many public school systems. The American Jewish Committee has been around since the early twentieth century. Its mission has always been to fight a legal battle so that all people may enjoy basic human rights. The American Jewish Congress is also a fighter for equality, active in the civil rights movement of the 1950s and 1960s, and continues to pursue equal right issues in the United States today.

The Mitzvah of Pikuach Nefesh

The issues of public health, hygiene, and medical practice date back to early Judaism. In the narrowest sense, they all deal with the sanctity of life. In Jewish tradition, human life is so importance that anything else is secondary to saving an individual. Those who observe Shabbat strictly may break their observance if someone's life is danger. Those who keep kosher may eat non-kosher foods if it will save their lives. Even if there is only a possibility of danger to human life, all efforts must be made to eliminate that danger.

Here are just a couple of examples that show how important it is to save a human life.

> Rabbi Shimon ben Menassia says: "The children of Israel shall keep the Sabbath." The Torah says to desecrate one Sabbath so that one may live to observe many Sabbaths.
>
> —Yoma 85b

> According to the great teacher Shmuel: Since an open wound is dangerous, one may violate the Sabbath for it.
>
> —Avodah Zarah 28a

While the mitzvah of pikuach nefesh usually deals with illnesses, it arises in other instances as well. If a person is in any sort of life-threatening situation, pikuach nefesh dictates that everything must be done to save his or her life.

Again, this lesson dates back centuries and can be found in the Talmud.

> Where do we learn that one who sees a person drowning in a river, or being mauled by an animal, or being attacked by robbers, is bound to save that person? From Leviticus 19:16, which teaches, "Do not stand idly by your neighbor's blood."
>
> —Sanhedrin 73a

By the same token, this mitzvah also means that you should not consciously place yourself or others in life-threatening situations. In other words, attempting to jump Niagara Falls on a motorcycle is in direct contradiction to the spirit of pikuach nefesh.

Where There's a Will, There's a Way

In the United States, some very different ways of fulfilling the mitzvah of pikuach nefesh have been developed. New York City is known for its sights and sounds, including sirens. Among the sirens one hears on New York's streets are of those of Hatzoloh, a private ambulance service run by the Jewish community, with mainly Orthodox volunteer emergency medical technicians. Hatzoloh is funded by communal donations from synagogues, other Jewish organizations, and individuals. It responds to any emergency call it receives, whether the person in need of help is Jewish or not.

Three Israeli stamps honoring the Magen David Adom. Magen David Adom means "Red Magen David" and is the equivalent of the American Red Cross.

הַצָּלָה

Jewish Ambulance Service

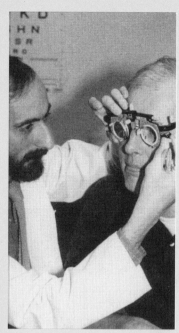

The Jewish Guild for the Blind is dedicated to pikuach nefesh. The Guild provides eye examinations and rehabilitation sessions for the visually-impaired. Restoring an individual's sight enhances the person's quality of life.

חֶסֶד שֶׁל אֱמֶת
respectful treatment
of the dead

Giving of Yourself

Jay Feinberg is a young man who desperately needed a bone transplant in order to live. The Jay Feinberg Foundation was set up to try to find a match for him. Over the course of a few years, thousands of American Jews found out about his plight through their synagogues and other Jewish organizations. Thousands of them volunteered, standing in line for hours at makeshift labs, to see if they might be the right match for a bone marrow transplant. Everyone who volunteered is now listed in the bone marrow donor bank and can get a call any time a match is found. They are willing to undergo removal of some bone marrow which would then be given to person in need, hopefully saving that individual's life.

In 1995, a matching donor was found for Jay Feinberg. The foundation set up in his name still exists to help others who need this medical help. When a match is found, and the donation takes place, it is done anonymously. Neither the donor nor the recipient knows who the other is. Their identities are kept secret for one year. Why do you think that is? Look back at the chapter on tzedakah and see how the different levels of giving and receiving can be applied to transplants.

Yet another way of fulfilling the mitzvah of pikuah nefesh can be undertaken by every adult who drives a car. Adults can choose to have an organ donor tag placed on their driver's license. This means that in case they die in an accident, they allow their organs to be used to save other lives. Presently, there are thousands of people in need of transplants: hearts, lungs livers. Many die because not enough people are willing to become organ donors. Organ donation is a twentieth-century addition to the mitzvah of pikuah nefesh.

A Living Memorial

Alisa Flatow was a twenty-year-old college student from New Jersey whose life ended tragically at the hands of terrorists in the Gaza Strip. Her parents were determined to bring some good out of their mourning. They donated her organs for medical transplants.

Thanks to their decision, six Israelis got another chance at life. (Unfortunately, two later died.) A number of Israelis were surprised by the decision to donate. They wrongly assumed that it is against Judaism to permit the use of organs for transplants. This concept is based on another mitzvah, hesed shel emet, which requires respectful treatment and swift burial of a corpse. Actually, all the major movements in American Judaism encourage organ donation. The leaders of modern Orthodox, Conservative, and Reform Judaism have all referred to organ donation as a mitzvah that will save lives, an act of pikuah nefesh.

Choose Life

The Talmud presents a challenging problem to the mitzvah of saving a life. In Bava Metzia 62a, the following scenario is presented: You are one of two people stranded in the desert. There is only enough water for one person to survive. What do you do? Rabbi Ben Peturah said that it is not fair to choose one life over the other, both persons should share the water. Rabbi Akiva disagreed. He said that you should save your own life first, and therefore not share the water. In the Talmud, the opinion of Rabbi Akiva was followed. Do you agree with this? How would you fulfill the mitzvah of pikuah nefesh in the same situation?

Keren Or is a state-of-the-art residential center in Jerusalem devoted to the care of blind or low-visioned children who are also physically or mentally disabled.

Dr. Richard Hodes, JDC's Medical Director in Ethiopia, gives medical treatment to a Rwandan child in the Kibumba refugee camp. Dr. Hodes led the JDC medical team sent to Goma, Zaire, in response to the crisis in Rwanda. (Photo: JDC)

Teachings from Tradition

One who causes the loss of even one life, it is as if that person caused the loss of an entire world, and one who saves one life, it is as if that person saved an entire world.

<Sanhedrin 37a>

One does not take a life in order to save a life

<Sanhedrin 72b>

Your life	חַיֶּיךָ
takes precedence	קוֹדְמִין
over your friend's life	לְחַיֵּי חֲבֵרֶךָ

<Bava Metzia 62a>

פִּדְיוֹן שְׁבוּיִים

Pidyon Shevuyim: Redeeming Captives

What do you do when you get bored? Do you go out and play, read, or enjoy a video game? Maybe you just close your eyes and imagine an adventure. For hundreds of years, people who dreamed of adventure sailed the seven seas. If you wanted to travel from one country to another you had to go by water. Ocean voyages were long and dangerous. People who sailed the sea had many fears: sickness, storms, sea monsters, or falling off the edge of the world. The biggest fear was pirates.

Pirates in small, speedy ships often attacked slower ships that were weighed down with cargo. They would steal the goods and capture the passengers. Despite our image of prisoners walking the planks, this did not happen very often. Usually, pirates wanted to get rid of their prisoners as soon as possible. They did this in exchange for money. This was called ransom.

Too many merchant ships loaded with goods from India and the Mediterranean had been captured by pirates. Things got so bad that in 1492, a sailor named Christopher Columbus set out to find a route that would avoid the pirates. He was looking for a new route to India.

Astrolabe with Hebrew lettering, made by a Jewish astronomer for Alfonso, king of Castile.

nnmer⁹ annornz	nomina mensiuz	dies	digiti	feria	bore	minu	finis eclipsis bore	minu
Tab eclipsis luminariuz et primo de sole
1403	octob	10	9	5	0	0	1	20
1502	septeb	30	8		17	28	19	12
1506	Julii	20	3	2	1	49	3	3
1513	martii	7	4	1	23	40	1	9
1518	Junii	7	10	2	18	22	19	17
1524	Iannaz	23	9	2	3	12	4	6

Tabla de eclipsibus lune
1494	septeb	14	17	1	17	5	2	33
1497	Iannaz	18	1	4	3	50	7	18
1500	noueb	5	13	5	10	17	13	30
1501	maii	2	10	1	15	33	19	6
1502	octob	15	14	7	10	15	12	9
1504	febzuz	20	16	1	10	47	4	13
1505	aug⁹	14	15	1	5	41	9	6
1508	Junii	12	23	2	15	21	19	0
1509	Junii	2	7	7	9	29	2	3
1511	octob	6	13	1	9	11	2	26
1514	Iannaz	29	16	1	14	20	16	3
1515	Iannaz	10	16	7	5	0	6	42
1516	Julii	13	14	1	10	10	12	30
1519	noueb	6	20	1	5	50	6	48

A chart from the perpetual almanac of Abraham Zacuto, Spanish astronomer whose books were studied by Columbus. The eclipse of the moon on February 29, 1504, is listed.

Star Track

In medieval times, Jews were very active in the field of astronomy. This was especially true in Moslem Spain, where Jews pursued all the sciences. For many Jews, astronomy was tied in with cartography, the science of map-making.

Jews served as intermediaries between East and West in the transmission of information, including astronomy. They translated astronomical information from the languages of the East to those of the West. A Jewish scholar named Sind ben Ali helped compile the Alfonsine astronomical tables in the ninth century.

The astrolabe, an instrument for determining a ship's location based on readings of the positions of the sun and certain stars, was brought to Europe in the eleventh century by Jewish intermediaries. They improved the instrument in several important way, including the use of metal instead of wood, allowing for more precise measurements.

Jacob ben Machir (also known as Prophatius) invented another navigational instrument, the quadrant of Israel. Abraham Zacuto compiled invaluable tables of navigational information for King Pedro IV of Portugal. These were translated into Latin by Joseph Vecinho and were used by Columbus. Levi ben Gershon (14th cent.), known as Magister Leo de Bagnolas, worked on an instrument called Jacob's staff which measures the angular separation between two celestial bodies. Translated into Latin, his written work was used by Columbus, Vasco da Gama, Magellan, and other famous explorers.

As Columbus headed west, the pirate problem continued in the east. Many of the pirates' victims were Jews. These Jews weren't looking for adventure, they were merchants carrying goods from country to country. They traveled the fastest way possible, by sea. The pirates were waiting for ships, stealing the cloth, spices, and other goods they carried. They also took the merchants prisoner.

For Jews, this was a terrible problem. Nothing could be worse than to have an innocent person held captive. Since the captors were intent on getting their money one way or another, there was always the fear that an unransomed hostage might be sold as a slave.

The Hazards of Traveling

Many people are afraid to travel. Some don't like to fly, others avoid trains, ships, or cars. This is not something new, although traveling is a lot safer today than in other centuries. Traveling used to be considered so dangerous that there is a special prayer to be said before setting out on a journey. The Tefillat Haderech (prayer for a journey) can be found in many Siddurim. As part of the evening service, a prayer called Hashkivenu is said. This prayer asks for God's protection at night, "Shield us from every enemy." Night was a particularly hazardous time for travelers, even for a short trip such as that from synagogue to home after an evening service.

Jewish sources give us guidance on what to do when traveling:

1. Before leaving on a journey, give tzedakah.
2. Get permission from the town leaders so that they may bless you on a successful journey. And take some people to accompany you (out of town).
3. When accompanying someone else, wait until you can't see them anymore.
4. Always take some bread along, even for a short trip.
5. If you are going to stay at an inn for the night, make sure to arrive before sunset; the next day, try to depart at sun rise.
6. Do not eat a lot while on a trip.
7. When eating, make sure your innkeeper is right eous and trustworthy (regarding the food given you).

—Kitzur Shulchan Aruch 68:5

Over hundreds of years, in different communities, rabbis taught the mitzvah of pidyon shevuyim, freeing the captives. Some rabbis said that it was a greater mitzvah than helping the poor. It was considered so important to free hostages that if anyone was held for ransom, tzedakah money set aside for the poor or for building a synagogue had to be used to obtain his or her freedom.

תְּפִילַת הַדֶּרֶךְ
prayer for a safe journey

הַשְׁכִּיבֵנוּ
evening prayer

Israel has provided homes for Russian and Oriental Jews who were held as shevuyim by despotic regimes. These two ex-hostages, with all their belongings in hand, are going to their new home in Israel.

The meeting place of the Council of Four Lands in Lublin in the sixteenth and seventeenth centuries.

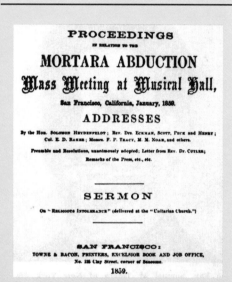

In 1858 Papal Guards kidnapped 6-year-old Edgar Mortara from his home in Bologna, Italy. The church officials decreed that Edgar must be brought up as a Catholic. In spite of mass protests by Jewish and non-Jewish citizens, the child was never returned to his parents.

Tombstone of Rabbi Meir of Rothenburg in the old Jewish cemetery of Worms

The Mitzvah of *Pidyon Shevuyim*

Throughout history, Jewish communities set up special groups to fulfill the mitzvah of pidyon shevuyim. In Alexandria, Egypt, from the ninth to the twelfth century, special fundraising was done just for this purpose. In seventeenth-century Italy, a rabbi named Samuel ben Abraham Aboab set up a pidyon shevuyim fund. In 1643, this money was used to ransom an entire community of Jews held captive by the Swedes.

Not all captives were taken at sea. At times pirates went ashore to kidnap people and hold them for ransom. In some cases people were put in jail for crimes they had not committed. The ruler would let them go only if a ransom was paid. This was a big problem for Jews in Europe who were falsely accused of committing crimes against Christians. From the sixteenth to the eighteenth century, there were two Jewish organizations responsible for ransoming Jews in Eastern Europe. One, in Poland, was called the Council of Four Lands; the other, in Lithuania, was the Council of the Lands.

Some Jews opposed the idea of ransoming captives in certain cases. One of them was Rabbi Meir ben Baruch of Rothenburg, the most outstanding rabbi of thirteenth-century Germany. When Rudolph I became emperor, he decided that everything the Jews owned really belonged to him. To prove this, he put a special tax on the Jews. Rabbi Meir and thousands of others fled. Unfortunately, someone recognized Rabbi Meir. He was caught and imprisoned in 1286. The emperor was willing to let him go if the Jewish community would pay a ransom. Rabbi Meir did not allow the Jewish community to do this. He was afraid that paying the ransom would only encourage Rudolph to take more hostages. Do you think he was right? The community followed Rabbi Meir's advice and he died in prison. His body was ransomed fourteen years after his death, in 1307.

A Refugee Turns Rescuer

Because Jews were so often expelled from the places they lived in and forced to find new homes, they were rarely able to set down permanent roots in one place. The largest expulsion of this kind took place in Spain in 1492. The country's Jews were required to convert to Christianity or leave. Many fled; some remained, converting outwardly but practicing Judaism in secret. They were known as conversos (secret Jews). Even many of the conversos were eventually forced to leave. Where did they go? At first, some went right next door—to Portugal. Eventually the Inquisition caught up with them there.

Among the conversos who left Portugal in the sixteenth century was a woman named Beatrice de Luna. Born in 1510, she was a first-generation Portuguese converso; her husband had been a successful banker and gemstone merchant. After his death, she and her relatives were forced to flee to Flanders. Because the family was wealthy, it was able to do things that other families couldn't. Beatrice and her brother-in-law used their wealth to help other Portuguese conversos to escape.

In 1543 Beatrice was forced to flee from Flanders and settled in Italy. Here she was denounced as a practicing Jew by her sister! Beatrice de Luna had friends in high places and was saved from imprisonment by a Turkish diplomat. From that time on, she lived openly as a Jew, using her Jewish name of Gracia Nasi.

Doña Gracia, known as "La Señora," continued to help other Jews, organizing the escape of conversos from Portugal. She also gave money to scholars and set up schools of Jewish studies. Doña Gracia moved once more in her life, leaving Ferrara, Italy, and moving to Constantinople, where she died in 1569. The Jewish community was so grateful for her efforts that two books were dedicated to her during her lifetime, one of them the Ferrara Spanish Bible. A synagogue in Constantinople was also named after her.

War and Peace

War often creates situations where the mitzvah of pidyon shevuyim is fulfilled. A number of organizations founded to help war refugees have also found themselves helping civilians to escape from wartorn countries. One such group is the Joint Distribution Committee (JDC), founded in 1914 to help

Portrait medal of
Doña Gracia Nasi, 1556

Joint Distribution JDC

Benjamin Franklin Peixotto
(1834–1890)
Leading Jewish citizen who was president of B'nai B'rith, consul to Bucharest, Rumania, and consul also in France. In Rumania he tried to help persecuted Jews.

This Yemenite family, brought to Israel during Operation Magic Carpet, was first lodged in a temporary camp called a *maabarah*. After a period of orientation the family was transferred to a farm settlement. The Yemenites have a love for the land and quickly became successful farmers. They mastered modern methods of farming and became an important social and economic asset to the State of Israel.

Jewish refugees in World War I. It is called the Joint because it is actually made up of three groups set up for this purpose at about the same time. Among other things, the Joint sent food to Jews in Turkish-held Palestine and aided Jews in Central and Eastern Europe who had been forced to leave their homes during the war and in its aftermath. During World War II, the Joint worked hard to get Jews out of Nazi-held territories, including the 1944 rescue of two trainloads of Jews from Hungary. The JDC managed to save 81,000 Jewish lives during the Holocaust. After World War II, the Joint concentrated on helping Holocaust victims find new homes in Israel and elsewhere. The JDC is still active in war-torn countries.

Fulfilling the Mitzvah Today

Today, the mitzvah of pidyon shevuyim means helping Jews who are in trouble in many parts of the world. This mitzvah has been used to free Jews living in countries where they are not allowed to be openly Jewish. At times it has meant helping Jews escape when they have been caught in a war. The money for pidyon shevuyim comes from Jews everywhere. In the United States it is collected by a national organization called the United Jewish Appeal, which distributes the funds

Some of the founders of the Joint Distribution Committee. Seated at the left is Felix M. Warburg, philanthropist and first Joint chairman.

to a number of agencies. Individual organizations such as the Joint Distribution Committee do their own fundraising.

During the 1970s and 1980s Jews around the world fought to help Jews leave the former Soviet Union. This project was known as Operation Exodus. Today, money is being used to help free Jews who are caught in the chaos of Eastern European nations created when the Soviet Union fell apart.

Newly arrived Russian immigrants.

A dramatic example of pidyon shevuyim took place on Memorial Day weekend in 1991. In the space of one weekend, 14,000 Jews were flown from Ethiopia to Israel. This was known as Operation Solomon. In Israel, these Jews were reunited with family members who had managed to escape a few years earlier during Operation Moses.

The tzedakah collected to help Jews in need is used to fly them out of dangerous areas, and to provide them with food, shelter, medicine, and education. It is meant to get them out of danger and help them start new lives in freedom and security.

A demonstration by Jewish activists in front of the Russian embassy.

Teachings from Tradition

Ransoming prisoners is a great mitzvah.

<Bava Batra 8b>

Death by the sword is a terrible death, hunger is worse still, and captivity is worst of all.

<Bava Batra 8b>

You shall proclaim	וּקְרָאתֶם
liberty	דְּרוֹר
throughout the land	בָּאָרֶץ
for all its inhabitants.	לְכָל־יֹשְׁבֶיהָ

<Vayikra 25:10>

The Liberty Bell in Philadelphia. The inscription on the bell is from the third book of the Bible, Leviticus 25:10, reading "Proclaim liberty throughout the land, for all its inhabitants."

אַהֲבַת צִיּוֹן

Ahavat Ziyyon:
Love for the Land of Israel

People take trips for many reasons. Sometimes you go on vacation. If there is a holiday, you might use the opportunity to visit relatives. Some people travel frequently for business reasons. There is a special journey that is taken for religious reasons. It is called a pilgrimage. This is the journey of a religious person to a sacred place. A Catholic visiting the Vatican and a Moslem traveling to Mecca are on pilgrimages. For Jews, the land of Israel and the city of Jerusalem have always been a core part of religious belief. In Psalm 137 this belief is put into words by the exiles in Babylon, who had been forced to leave their homeland after Jerusalem was destroyed:

> How can we sing a song of Adonai on foreign soil?
> If I forget you, O Jerusalem, let my right hand cease to
> function, let my tongue stick to the roof of my mouth if I
> stop thinking of you, if I do not set Jerusalem above my
> highest joy.

From the Mississippi River to the Jordan River
Many people keep journals of their trips. In the United States, the writer Mark Twain published a journal of his world travels in 1869. He called it *The Innocents Abroad.* Among his adventures are a few chapters describing his visit to the land

Three times a year (Sukkot, Pesach, and Shavuot) the Jews of ancient Israel would march on foot to the Holy Temple in Jerusalem. Today in modern Israel, the age-old ceremony is reenacted. Here pilgrims ascend Mount Zion to the blowing of the shofars.

Livnot U'Lehibanot enhances the Israel experience for New York-area youth in hopes of opening the door to a lifetime of Jewish involvement. The three-month work/study program is one of many initiatives supported through UJA-Federation's Legacy Fund Program.

• 39

Jews of Tiberias, 1894.

The tomb of Rambam in Tiberias. He arrived in Eretz Yisrael with his family in 1165 and settled in Akko. However, because of disturbances due to the crusader invasions, he left and settled in Egypt. Eventually, he became Saladin's court physician. He died in Egypt, and at his request was buried in Tiberias.

As in ancient days, Jews all over the world celebrate the holiday of Sukkot by blessing the lulav and etrog.

of Israel. It was more than a sightseeing trip, it was a pilgrimage. He was visiting sites important to him as a Christian. Some of the places he visited were sites holy to Jews.

> A fast walker could go outside the walls of Jerusalem and walk entirely around the city in one hour. I do not know how else to make one understand how small it is. . . . The streets are roughly and badly paved, and are tolerably crooked. . . . I have several times seen cats jump across the street from one shed to the other when they were out calling. The cats could have jumped double the distance without extraordinary exertion. I mention this to give an idea of how narrow the streets are.

Even after the beginning of the Diaspora and the destruction of the Second Temple, there was always a Jewish presence in the land of Israel. Throughout the centuries, many Jews had the goal of living in Israel. Some, despite great hardships, went there either on pilgrimages or to stay. This too was described by Mark Twain in his comments on the city of Tiberias:

> . . . and for three hundred years Tiberias was the metropolis of the Jews in Palestine. It has been the abiding-place of many learned and famous Jewish rabbins [rabbis]. They lie buried here, and near them lie also twenty-five thousand of their faith who traveled far to be near them while they lived and lie with them when they died.

The Mitzvah of Ahavat Ziyyon
The special place that Israel holds in Judaism is known as *ahavat ziyyon*, the love of Zion. Zion is one of the biblical names of Jerusalem, which by extension refers to all of Israel. In the Siddur we recite special prayers for the peace of Israel and Jerusalem. Many of our holidays are tied in with the agricultural calendar of ancient Israel. These include the pilgrimage holidays of Pesach, Sukkot, and Shavuot, when the ancient Israelites would travel to the Temple in Jerusalem. Tu BiShevat is also directly tied in with the agricultural calendar of ancient Israel. Today, the modern holidays of Yom Hazikaron (Israeli Memorial Day), *Yom Ha-Atzma'ut* (Israeli Independence Day), and Yom Yerushalayim (Jerusalem Day) give Jews around the world an opportunity to demonstrate their love for Israel.

40 •

Throughout history, the love of Israel and Jerusalem has always been a central Jewish belief. Jews from all countries sought to settle in the land of Israel. Those who could not settle there had a lifelong goal of visiting Israel and Jerusalem.

Settling in the land of Israel is a mitzvah. It is called aliyah, meaning "to go up." This is the same word we use when we are called up to the Torah. Both acts symbolize rising to a higher spiritual level.

Jews who do not live there show their love for Israel in many ways. There have always been organizations that collect money to support those who live in Israel. Throughout history, Jews living outside of Israel have considered it their duty to help the Jews in Israel, and tzedakah was raised for this purpose wherever Jews lived.

Today many organizations raise money for Israel. The United Jewish Appeal, one of the major American fundraising organizations, contributes money to Israel through a branch organization, the United Israel Appeal. There are special appeals for many special programs, such as those to help resettle Ethiopian or Russian Jews.

The women's Zionist organization, Hadassah, was created to meet the health needs of all the people living in the land of Israel. Today, Hadassah Hospital in Jerusalem is one of the most advanced hospitals in the Middle East; it continues to serve the health needs of both Jews and Arabs.

A New Career

Henrietta Szold was fifty years old and had achieved much when she settled in Jerusalem after a visit there in 1909. She had already been a student at the all-male Jewish Theological Seminary, a teacher, and an editor in addition to setting up evening schools to help new immigrants coming to America. She was the founder of Hadassah, the Women's Zionist Organization of America, which grew to become the largest Jewish organization in the history of the United States.

After her initial visit to Israel, Henrietta Szold decided that the Jewish community needed specific help, mostly health care. Because of her efforts, the philanthropist Nathan Straus financed a medical unit in Palestine in 1913.

Hadassah took on a new mission as well. It concentrated on providing medical care to the community in Palestine.

Two Israeli stamps commemorating the 20th anniversary of Hadassah.

In 1912, Henrietta Szold founded Hadassah. Her work took her on many trips to Palestine, and her organization also founded such institutions as the American Daughters of Zion Nurses Settlement. These women are American Jewish nurses.

Archbishop Joseph Cardinal Bernardin of Chicago, on his first visit to Israel, planted a tree for Catholic-Jewish dialogue at the dedication of a forest in his name on Mount Turan. The new woodland was a gift from Chicago's Jewish Community Relations Council to the cardinal for his long-standing commitment to interfaith understanding and to free Soviet Jewry.

**World Zionist Organization
WZO**

**Zionist Organization of America
ZOA**

**Jewish National Fund
JNF**

Today, in addition to the Hadassah Hospital in Jerusalem, it operates numerous clinics providing medical care around the country.

These successes were not enough for Henrietta Szold. During World War II she ran a special program that rescued children from Nazi Europe. Known as the Youth Aliyah program, it brought these children to Israel. Many of them were orphans. Youth Aliyah, through the Jewish Agency, set up many different programs to help the young refugees, including special youth villages, schools, and kibbutz placements. Youth Aliyah programs still exist today. They are very successful in giving refugee children who have had traumatic experiences a new, safe, and secure home in Israel.

Most Hebrew school students are familiar with the Jewish National Fund. The money collected in the blue-and-white boxes in religious schools is used to plant forests in Israel. In the years before the State of Israel was founded, JNF money was used to purchase land which was then settled by the chalutzim (pioneers).

Today, there are countless other organizations, some highly specialized, that receive tzedakah to be used in Israel. Some are affiliated with one of the religious denominations, others are political in nature. There are groups that work for the environment in Israel, groups that support the arts, and organizations that help Israelis with special needs. The support given by Jews outside of Israel is an expression of ahavat ziyyon.

The Many Faces of Zionism

Zionism is the liberation movement of the Jewish people, founded by Theodor Herzl. Zionists believe that the Jewish people have a right to govern themselves in the Jewish homeland, Israel. In 1897, Herzl founded the World Zionist Organization (WZO). The Jewish National Fund was added in the early 1900s, in order to raise money for the purchase of land in Israel.

Today there are many Zionist organizations, reflecting all the varieties that exist within Judaism itself, from the completely secular to the very religious. The American Zionist Foundation (AZF) is an umbrella group for several Zionist organizations. One of its branches is the American Zionist

Youth Foundation (AZYF), which focuses on Zionist activities for high school and college age youth. The Zionist Organization of America (ZOA) supports the Likud party in Israel. The Labor party has its supporters in the United States as well.

The Reform movement formed the Association of Reform Zionists of America (ARZA). Part of its mission is to fight for religious pluralism in Israel, where Orthodox Judaism is the only accepted form of Jewish practice. MERCAZ is the Conservative movement's Zionist arm. Part of its mission is also to expand the rights of non-Orthodox Jews in Israel. Mizrachi, the Religious Zionists of America, is an Orthodox Zionist organization, representing the special interests of modern Orthodoxy in its Zionism.

Some people feel that support for Israel includes official American support. AIPAC, the American Israel Public Affairs Committee, is a lobbying organization, focusing on convincing members of Congress to pass legislation that helps Israel. Among the major issues are Israel's security and American foreign aid to Israel.

Putting Your Mouth Where Your Money Is

A number of Jews outside of Israel take the next step in showing ahavat ziyyon. They visit Israel. For some this is a short tourist excursion, for others it means buying a home there. Some people volunteer to work on a kibbutz, others look forward to waking up at 4:00 to work on an archaeological dig.

For many students, Israel is a popular place to spend a summer, a semester, or a year. There are special high school programs and college programs. Students learn Hebrew, explore the country, and take courses for credit back home. It is an unforgettable experience. All youth groups and denominations have special programs in Israel. Colleges and Hillel, the college student organization, can provide information about college programs. More and more families are setting aside money that would have been spent on a lavish Bar or Bat Mitzvah and, instead, using it to send the teenager to Israel.

The greatest way to express ahavat ziyyon is by making *aliyah*. This means accepting the obligation of living in Israel, becoming a citizen, serving in the Israel Defense Forces, pay-

**Association of Reform Zionists of America
ARZA**

**American Israel Public Affairs Committee
AIPAC**

Sabbath afternoon is a time for study and rest. Here, yeshiva students in Israel review their weekly lessons.

עֲלִיָּה
going up to Israel

צַהַ"ל
**Israel Defense Forces
IDF**

הָלֵל
Hillel

Israeli stamp conmemorating the 50th anniversary of the aliyah from Germany.

ing taxes and raising a family in Israel. It means choosing whether to live in a city, town, or kibbutz. It might also mean giving up certain career goals or changing careers in order to be able to work in Israel. For those interested in aliyah, organizations like the ZOA can help make the transition smoother.

Hands Across the Ocean

While making aliyah is a wonderful step to take, it is also difficult. Obviously, there is a new language and lifestyle to learn. All this can be very exciting. What can be most difficult is leaving people behind. Those who make aliyah usually have left many friends and relatives behind in the country of their birth.

In the United States and Canada, family members of olim (people who make aliyah) have created their own organization. This group is called Parents of North American Israelis (PNAI). Its members share the pride of knowing that their children have taken on a wonderful mitzvah. At the same time, they get together to deal with the sadness of not being able to see their children and grandchildren frequently. They are also actively involved in political issues concerning Israel.

People who live outside of Israel have come up with some creative ways to show ahavat ziyyon. There are people who fly EL Al, the Israeli airline, whenever they travel. Some individuals make it a special point to buy Israeli products, watch Israeli films, or listen to Israeli music. Many cable stations now carry weekly programs about Israel. Can you come up with an imaginative way to fulfill the mitzvah of ahavat ziyyon?

El-Al, the Israeli airline.

Teachings from Tradition

A land flowing with milk and honey.

<Devarim 6:3>

May the One Who causes peace in the heavens cause peace to reign on us and on all Israel.

<Siddur>

If you will it, it is no dream.

<Theodore Herzl>

If a land has a soul,
then Jerusalem
is the soul
of Israel.

אִם לָאָרֶץ נְשָׁמָה,
הֲרֵי יְרוּשָׁלַיִם
נִשְׁמָתָהּ
שֶׁל אֶרֶץ יִשְׂרָאֵל

<David Ben-Gurion>

גְּמִילוּת חֲסָדִים

Gemilut Hasadim:
Acts of Lovingkindness

The great drought and dust storms of 1934 ravaged a dozen states and enlarged the New Deal's relief problems. Above, Lamar, Colorado, at the height of "the blow."

Public Works Administration PWA

What do you do when a dream turns into a nightmare? This was a situation faced by many Americans in the 1930s. Their pioneering ancestors had gone west in the late 1800s to fulfill a dream. The Homestead Act had given them free land—as long as they stayed on it and cultivated it for five years.

By the 1930s, the dream had turned into a nightmare for those who had settled in the Great Plains. For decades, the homesteaders had raised cattle and planted wheat in the fine soil. Unfortunately, a cycle of droughts and downpours did not go well with the wheat that was planted. Topsoil was slowly being lost, and by the 1930s the wind was carrying away the soil as dust, darkening the sky and leaving piles of dirt on the farmhouses. For this reason, the Great Plains became known as the Dust Bowl.

The Dust Bowl was part of the Great Depression of the 1930s. In order to help the people who had no food, no work, and apparently no future, President Franklin D. Roosevelt came up with a series of programs. He called this the New Deal. Between 1933 and 1938, the president and Congress founded many new agencies. The most famous program was the Public Works Administration (PWA), which gave people an opportunity to work building roads, bridges, and government buildings, many of which are still in use today. It even

46 •

employed artists to decorate these structures and photographers to record the events.

What the New Deal programs ultimately did, was to give people who had nothing a chance to make something of themselves. In Judaism, this is the highest form of *tzedakah*, giving a person the opportunity for self-help. In this way, the recipients remain independent, have self-esteem because they are working, and receive training so they may continue to work without relying on help from others.

Jewish Farmers

It is not often that Jews are thought of as farmers. If you imagine a Jewish farmer, you probably think of a kibbutz worker. The United States has a history of Jewish farmers, including a few pioneers who took advantage of the Homestead Act in the nineteenth century. Some were successful, others not so lucky.

A group of pioneers from a Russian Jewish movement called Am Olam (Nation of the World) had as its goal training Jews to emigrate to America and earn their livings there as farmers. Unfortunately, many of these immigrants met with prejudice and incompetent administrators who settled them in non-fertile places such as Cotapaxi, Colorado, or the Dakota Territory.

More fortunate Am Olam members were sent to Vineland and Carmel, New Jersey. Jewish farmers played a very important role in southern and central New Jersey in this century. In fact, Jewish farmers who specialized in raising poultry are credited with making New Jersey the "white Leghorn capital of the world."

The Mitzvah of Gemilut Hasadim

The term *gemilut hasadim* means "acts of lovingkindness." It refers to a mitzvah a person does without expecting anything in return. It is hoped that any mitzvah that one performs is done for the sake of doing a mitzvah. Human nature being what it is, there might be a thought in the back of your mind that if you do something for someone, they will pay you back one day. In carrying out an act of gemilut hasadim, you do not know who receives the money or items you donate. You do not know how the recipient will use what you donate, and you

Farmers' synagogue in Toms River, New Jersey. The bulletin board lists the Jewish men and women who served in the armed forces in World War II.

עַם עוֹלָם

Nation of the World

Farmhouse of a Jewish settler in the Lasker Colony, Kansas, 1885. The farmhouse was constructed of sod.

גְּמִילוּת חֲסָדִים

acts of lovingkindness

• 47

Israeli stamp honoring social welfare workers

גְּמִילוּת חֶסֶד

Free Loan Society

The tradition of gemilut hasadim (free loans) is an ancient and honorable one. *Gemilut* means "doing kindness." This Jew in pre-Holocaust Poland is shown borrowing money from a free loan society.

have no say in the matter. The person receiving the donated money or items does not know who made the donation.

Why would you want to do something without letting other people know about it? Many times, a person who needs help is embarrassed to ask for it. A recipient who knows who has provided the help may feel in debt to the donor. If the recipient is one of your friends or neighbors, and knows you are the donor, he or she may feel inferior to you. Conversely, if you knew your donation went to a friend, you might feel superior to that person. It is very difficult to treat as equals those who help us or those we help. Gemilut hasadim provides the perfect opportunity for both the donor and the recipient to maintain their dignity.

But gemilut hasadim is an act that goes beyond donating money. This mitzvah encompasses much more than single acts of tzedakah. That is why it is considered so important in Jewish tradition.

> Our rabbis taught: In three ways gemilut hasadim is better than charity. Charity can be done only with one's money, gemilut hasadim can be done with one's being as well as one's money. Charity can only be given to the poor, gemilut hasadim can be given to rich and poor. Charity can be given only to the living, gemilut hasadim can be given to the living or the dead.

What can you do that would be of help to someone who is rich? What is an act of lovingkindness toward a person who has died?

Helping Those Who Help Themselves

Jewish communities throughout the ages established systems for allowing people to fulfill the mitzvah of gemilut hasadim. A popular way of accomplishing this is through a free loan society, also called a gemilut hesed society.

Those who are able make donations to the free loan society. People who find themselves in need apply, in confidence, for an interest-free loan. The loan can be used for many purposes. One family might need it to help pay the rent, another to help pay for school tuition, a third person to help pay for expensive medical treatment.

What must be kept in mind is that the money is a loan. Once they are in a better financial position, the recipients start

48 •

paying it back. Very few people do not pay back loans from gemilut hesed societies. The money that is paid back is then loaned to other people in need. By paying back the loan, those who were helped end up helping others. In this way, more and more people take part in the mitzvah of gemilut hasadim.

With the massive immigration of Jews to the United States, new groups were formed that fulfilled the mitzvah of gemilut hasadim. Many newcomers stayed together, settling in neighborhoods where earlier immigrants from their hometown had settled. They formed organizations called landsmanshaften that provided various forms of assistance to newcomers.

Strength in Numbers

Many landsmanshaften were originally synagogue groups, people who got together to pray. When they saw the great need of their landsmen, newcomers from the same town or region in Europe, they took on the role of benevolent societies, providing for the good of their people. As the immigrants settled, and dispersed around the country, most of these organizations eventually died out.

One such group is still going strong, however. It was founded at the same time as the other benevolent organizations, and eventually some of the smaller ones joined it. This organization is the Workmen's Circle. The Arbeiter Ring, as it is known in Yiddish, had a twofold purpose. It provided various forms of aid to immigrants, from loans to help with health and burial costs. It also promoted cultural and educational activities, especially those having to do with Yiddish. In the early 1900s it helped to develop the Jewish afternoon school, setting up numerous programs in areas of large Jewish population.

Unlike the landsmanshaften, the Workmen's Circle is a completely secular organization. As the name indicates, it was first and foremost concerned with workers, and had a socialist political leaning. In recent years, with the growing interest in the Yiddish language and culture, the Workmen's Circle has experienced a revival in providing educational and cultural programs, including Yiddish classes and discussion groups.

New Jewish arrivals in the United States could also turn to the Hebrew Immigrant Aid Society (HIAS). This group

קאָנסטיטושאָן
דער
...קאָמענעץ פּאָדאָלער...
...פּראָג. ליידיעם אסס'ן.

געגרינדעט דעם 16טען סעפּטעמבער, 1908

Title page of a landsmanshaft constitution. The Komenets Podolier Ladies Association, founded 1908.

**Abeiter Ring
(Workmen's Circle)**

קאָנסטיטוציאָן
— פון דיא —
יוניטעד קלאָטה-העט אונד
קעפּ מייקערס

אָף נאָרטה אַמעריקא

פעראייניגונג סיט דיא
אמעריקאן פעדערייישאָן אָף לייבאָר.

Yiddish constitution of the United Cloth Hat and Cap Makers Union of 1921.

**Hebrew Immigrant
Aid Society
HIAS**

Polish Jews before World War I asking advice about emigrating to the United States, at the information desk of the Hebrew Immigrant Aid Society in Warsaw.

**Jewish Vocational Services
JVS**

Israeli stamp honoring the centenary of ORT

**Society for Manual Work
ORT**

provided financial, educational, and moral support to many immigrants. Eventually, HIAS's focus on immigration led to its joining forces with the Joint Distribution Committee (see chap. 6) in its fight to help Jews emigrate from troubled lands.

Free loan societies are still found in cities where there are major Jewish communities. What do you do if you live in a small town? Some synagogues have their own free loan societies that operate in confidence, just like the ones in big cities. People in need can always turn to the rabbi or cantor for financial help. The money they are provided is usually given as a grant that only the rabbi or cantor knows about. It is taken from a special discretionary fund that each member of the clergy has specifically to help people in need. Once the crisis is over, the recipient often makes a donation to the fund to help others in need.

There is yet another way in which the Jewish community tries to help people establish themselves. This is done through Jewish Vocational Services (JVS). This organization provides job training, counseling, and networking. It teaches people how to prepare resumes and job applications. It has a listing of businesses that are looking for employees. JVS runs classes to help you improve your skills. These services are available to anyone in the Jewish community. They have been used by recent graduates, mothers getting back into the workforce, and people switching careers.

In recent years, Jewish Vocational Services has done much to help Russian immigrants find work in their new home. JVS has run classes on how to interview for a job. It has helped immigrants prepare resumes that summarize their work experience. It has even gotten Jewish business owners to make a special effort to hire and train immigrants.

Learning and Doing
The Jewish people have always believed that knowledge is the key to success. This does not mean that if you are real smart you will be wealthy. What it means is that learning helps you to support yourself, your family, and others in turn, thereby fulfilling the mitzvah of gemilut hasadim.

There is yet another organization that exists to train people to be self-sufficient. This group is called ORT, which is a short name for a long Russian name meaning "Society for

Manual Work" or "Society for Spreading Work." As the name implies, ORT exists to train people in vocational and technical fields.

It began in the 1880s in Russia in an attempt to develop new schools and open new occupations to Jews. ORT set up model farms and farming colonies. While at first it was a Russian Jewish organization, ORT eventually became a global Jewish group. Today it concentrates on providing technical training for Jewish communities in Africa, Asia, Europe, and the Americas. ORT has been especially helpful to Jews who have had to emigrate to new homes, helping them acquire new skills in order to earn a living. Today ORT no longer concentrates on farming skills. The educational focus has shifted to keep up with the modern world. ORT has branched out, and its schools now stress technological skills, including computer training.

These are just some of the ways that the Jewish community has tried to fulfill the mitzvah of gemilut hasadim. Every Jewish community is different. You know what is special about your community, and you know where the problems lie. Can you come up with some creative ways to solve some of its problems—ways where you help people without their knowing you are helping them? When you have accomplished this—say, by leaving groceries on a hungry person's doorstep, paying someone to mow your lawn when you can do it yourself, or even inviting a not-so-popular student to help you on a project—-you have fulfilled the mitzvah of gemilut hasadim. Perhaps this is why a well-known Jewish teaching reminds us: "The world is established by three things: Torah (study), service to God, and acts of gemilut hasadim."

The age-old tradition of tzedakah is practiced in many ways today. These youngsters, at Kfar Abraham, Israel, receive help through the Joint Distribution Committee.

Boys Town–Jerusalem

Established in 1948 to offer a comprehensive academic, religious and technical education to disadvantaged Israeli and immigrant boys from 45 countries, including Ethiopia, Iran, and most recently, Russia. Enrollment: Over 1,000 students from junior high school through academic and technical high school and a college of applied engineering. Programs include electronics, computer science, precision mathematics, computerized design and manufacturing, and other technological courses. One of the largest boarding schools in Israel, with a beautiful 18 -acre campus overlooking the city of Jerusalem. Ten thousand graduates in industry, education, science, technology, and spiritual leadership are making an outstanding contribution to Israel's development.

Boys Town Jerusalem

Teachings from Tradition

Deeds of lovingkindness are greater than charity, for it is said: "Sow for yourselves according to charity but reap according to your lovingkindness" (Hosea 10:12).

<Sukkah 49b>

When there is no truth, there is no hesed.

<Sefer HaMiddot, R. Nahman of Bratslav>

For the sake of hesed the world exists.

בִּשְׁבִיל הַחֶסֶד
הָעוֹלָם מִתְקַיֵּם

<attributed to Rashi, Pirke Avot 1>

מָעוֹת חִטִּים

Maot Hittim:
Wheat Money

Israeli stamp with End to Hunger theme.
The tab reads :
"I will not let you go hungry."

When talking about evolution, we think about dinosaurs, human beings, and every animal in-between. We never give much thought to the evolution of plants, even though the development of plants had much to do with the growth of civilization. Wheat and barley were domesticated in the Middle East as early as 8000 B.C.E. That's about one thousand years after goats were domesticated, the same time as sheep, and two thousand years before cattle. Being able to grow foodstuffs meant that there would be enough for people and their animals to eat, as well as raw materials of diverse kinds that could be used for textiles and other products.

Thanks to domestication, crops could be planted, and a small number of people was able to raise enough food to feed a larger group. This eventually led to the rise of cities. One of the earliest cities was the famous city of Jericho. It was thousands of years old before the biblical story about its walls tumbling down.

With domestication and a growing population came new problems. One of these problems still exists today. We don't all have the same amount of everything. For some people it is easy to get food, for others it is a constant struggle.

This is a familiar problem in the Bible. The biblical solution was for the farmers to set aside the corners of their fields and leave them untouched. Then people in need could go to the fields at harvest time and glean their own food. In this way, they were provided for and did not feel as though they were receiving a handout.

The most famous episode of gleaning takes place in the book of Ruth. Ruth, a Moabite woman, has come to Bethlehem with her mother-in-law, Naomi. They arrive at the time of the barley harvest. Since both are widowed and have no means of support, Ruth goes to the fields and gleans. She happens to glean in the field of a man named Boaz, who is most generous to her, and instructs his workers to leave extra produce for her to glean, without her realizing it. To find out why, read Ruth, chapter 2.

How Much Is Enough?

פֵּאָה

corner

The Hebrew word *peah* means "corner." It is the term used to designate the corner of the field that is to be left for the poor, orphaned, and widowed. While the idea of leaving the corners of the field to be gleaned by those in need is described in the Torah, the concept is so important that a section of the Mishnah is devoted to this mitzvah. Among the issues discussed in the Mishnah are: how much is enough? how big a portion of the field should be left for those in need?

מִשְׁנָה

Mishnah

The answer is found in Peah 1:2. The amount of peah should not be less than one-sixtieth of the whole crop. No definite amount is stated for peah; its area depends upon the size of the field, the number of poor people, and the extent of the standing crop. Showing insight into human nature, the Mishnah also states that the crops left for gleaning may not just be inferior crops. Why do you think this has to be stressed?

Another question asks what exactly has to be set aside for gleaning: is it anything that is planted in a field? The response is found in Peah 1:4. Whatever is used for food, looked after, grown from the soil, and completely harvested and stored is subject to peah. Grain and pulse (lentils, beans) fall under this principle.

One question to consider is why the items are left in the field. Why should those in need harvest the items themselves? Wouldn't it be easier for the farmer to harvest everything and then just hand out baskets of food? Look at Maimonides' mitzvah ladder again and you will figure out the answer to this question.

The Mitzvah of Maot Hittim

There are many mitzvot that have to do with feeding the poor. A very special one occurs on Pesach. It is important because Pesach can be a very difficult time. Observant Jews must get rid of all the regular food they eat during the year, and only purchase or prepare food that is kosher for Pesach. This can be very expensive. If a person is on a limited budget, it is even more difficult. How can someone of limited means observe Pesach if she or he does not have the proper food?

The mitzvah of maot hittim sees to it that all Jews in need can celebrate Pesach. The term maot hittim means "wheat money." It refers to the wheat flour that is used to make the Passover matzah. Historically, any Jew who lived in a community for twelve months had one of two obligations. A person who was financially able was obligated to give money to the community for maot hittim. A person who was struggling financially was obligated to receive maot hittim in order to celebrate Passover.

In the Middle Ages, this became a very formal process in many Jewish communities. The rabbi and seven leading members of the community drew up a list of all the residents in town. The list consisted of two columns: those who would give and those who would receive wheat money.

While this formality no longer exists, the mitzvah of maot hittim is still in effect. Traditionally, people will make a special donation to the synagogue for the maot hittim fund. This money is set aside to be given to those who need financial help in preparing for Pesach. Some synagogues now have special food drives and distribute kosher for Passover foods to members of the community in need.

מָעוֹת חִטִּים
wheat money

מַתָּנוֹת לָאֶבְיוֹנִים
gifts to the poor

• 55

The holiday of Pesach teaches us other ways to help the hungry. At the beginning of the Seder, we recite these words from the Haggadah: "Let all who are hungry come and eat." It is traditional to have a place set for anyone who might be in need and comes off the street to share in the Seder.

On Purim we are told to give gifts to the poor (*matanot la'evyonim*), in order to make sure that they too can enjoy the festival. The custom of helping the needy is carried out on Shabbat as well. Inviting a needy person to share a Shabbat meal enhances the Shabbat celebration for all concerned.

"Cutting Corners"

Since we are no longer a farming society, we have had to come up with creative ways of feeding the needy. The challenge is to do it in a way that does not embarrass those who are hungry. More and more synagogues collect food for homeless shelters and food pantries. In some synagogues, there is a box at the entrance. You can donate food every time you walk into temple! Sometimes, at a special event, the cost of admission will be a can of food. If you want to go to the Purim carnival you have to bring a can of tuna, a box of pasta, or some other nonperishable item.

Many temples actively participate in local soup kitchens and food pantries. Synagogue members sign up to work at these places on a regular basis. The first Tuesday of the month might be your temple's night, the first Thursday would be the responsibility of another synagogue.

Some synagogues still do a type of maot hittim food collection. In preparation for Pesach, members are asked to bring in their hametz, items such as pasta that are not kosher for Passover. These items are then donated to a food pantry.

A number of congregations also do a major food drive on Yom Kippur. Why do you think they associate the mitzvah of feeding the hungry with the High Holy Days? What other holidays lend themselves to this mitzvah?

There is a growing movement to remember the hungry at all our events. A simple way of doing this was created by an organization called Mazon. This organization, whose name is

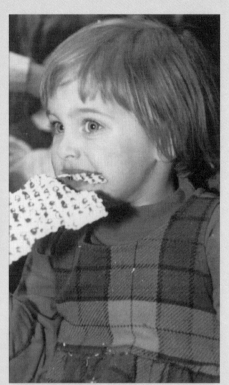

The Budapest Jewish community celebrates Passover at a Seder in the JDC-supported community center.

מָזוֹן

nutrition

Hebrew for "nutrition," suggests that we impose a three percent tax on ourselves. For example, your parents would take the bill for feeding your guests at your Bar or Bat Mitzvah. They would figure out what three percent of the total comes to. Then they would write a check for that amount and send it to Mazon.

This type of self-taxation has a long Jewish tradition. In the Middle Ages, Jews who were well off would set aside tzedakah money whenever they indulged themselves. For example, there are records of Jews who taxed themselves a gold piece for every additional glass of wine they had at a meal. This money was given to charity.

Your Tax Dollars at Work

Because of this self-taxation at Jewish activities, Mazon has become a major instrument for feeding the hungry in the United States. Mazon receives money from Jews all over the country. This money represents thousands of celebrations, from baby-namings to sisterhood dinners, from youth group pizza parties to family birthday celebrations.

JDC programs help keep Jewish culture alive in more than 50 countries worldwide. Sometimes they supply kosher food to local canteens in Eastern European countries so elderly Jews can live out their remaining years in dignity.

Mazon takes this money and distributes it to numerous organizations around the country. These are groups that feed the poor in all parts of the United States. One recipient could be a soup kitchen that feeds hundreds in New York City. Another group might be a small homeless shelter in the Midwest. A third group helps provide breakfasts for hungry schoolchildren in San Diego. Any group in the United States that feeds the hungry can apply to Mazon for financial help. Though it is a Jewish organization, Mazon provides funding for all groups that provide food for the hungry. This organization has created an imaginative way of leaving the corners of the fields for those who are hungry.

Providing food is one of the most basic mitzvot. In a large society like ours, basic nutritional needs are easily overlooked. There is so much else to deal with: what clothes to buy, what movies to watch. We forget that not everyone is equally fortunate. While we may worry about getting the latest video game, someone else is worrying about getting their next meal.

There is a Jewish teaching that without flour there is no Torah. This means that if we are hungry, we cannot fulfill the teachings of the Torah. Judaism teaches that if we let others go hungry, we are not fulfilling the Torah. Torah and Judaism have always provided creative ways to make sure that people do not go hungry. As a member of the Jewish community, you too have to come up with creative ways to help those who do not have a sandwich to take to school.

Teachings from Tradition

When you reap the harvest of your field and overlook a sheaf in the field, do not go back to get it; it shall go to the stranger, the orphan, and the widow, in order that Adonai your God may bless you in all that you do. When you beat down the fruit of your olive trees, do not go over them again; that shall go to the stranger, the orphan and the widow. When you gather the grapes of your vineyard, do not pick it over again; that shall go to the stranger, the orphan and the widow.

<Devarim 24:19–21>

They were to observe them* (the fourteenth and the fifteenth of Adar) as days of feasting and joy, an occasion for sending gifts to each other, and presents to the poor.

<Esther 9:22>

Let all who are hungry	כָּל־דִכְפִין
come	יֵיתֵי
and eat.	וְיֵיכוֹל

<Haggadah>

הִדּוּר פְּנֵי זָקֵן

Hiddur P'nai Zaken:
Respect for the Elderly

Norman Vaughan was a twenty-two-year-old dog-sled driver who accompanied Admiral Byrd to the South Pole in 1928. The admiral named a mountain after the young "musher" on an expedition in the 1930s. Vaughan missed out on that adventure. He always dreamed of going back to Antarctica and climbing the mountain that carries his name—and he did.

On December 16, 1994, Norman Vaughan reached the top of the 10,300-foot mountain. It took him eight days to scale the peak. He was carrying 75 pounds of gear, facing wind gusts of 40 knots and subfreezing temperatures.

When he reached the top of Mount Vaughan, Norman Vaughan was three days short of his eighty-ninth birthday. From the mountain he made the following statement: "A message I wish to bring to everyone is to dream big and 'dare to fail.' All of us have more inside us than we believe possible. I am now ready for my next challenge."

Never Too Old

Many people throughout history have accepted the challenge of aging as an opportunity to try new things. One such per-

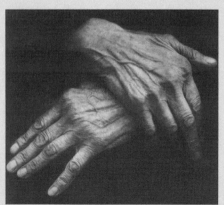

These are the hands that rocked the cradle, fed the children, and created the wonderful world in which we live.

son, who changed careers at the age of seventy, was the artist Shalom Moskovitz. He is better known as Shalom of Safed (the town in northern Israel where he lives).

Born in 1887, Shalom Moskovitz spent most of his life as a watchmaker, silversmith, and stonemason. Encouraged by an artist friend, he began to develop his artistic ability long after most people retire.

Shalom of Safed is known for his paintings of biblical stories. His paintings can be described as murals, showing a story line by line or panel by panel. He is known for the brilliant colors and repeated forms in his pictures.

In his second career as a painter, Shalom of Safed became famous, and his pictures hang in galleries around the world. Perhaps your temple has a poster of a Shalom of Safed painting.

The Mitzvah of Hiddur Penai Zaken

When we think about the elderly, the mountain-climbing Norman Vaughan is the last image that comes to mind. How do you imagine an elderly person? Is it someone with no teeth? A person who walks with a cane? A person who has trouble hearing or understanding what you say? At what age does someone become old? How do you know that someone is old?

Our images of elderly people lead us to act toward them in a certain way. Sometimes we are impatient because they are too slow or because we have to repeat things. Other times we feel that they are in a different world and don't understand us.

Judaism teaches us that our first impression of the elderly are often wrong. That is why we have a mitzvah called *hiddur p'nai zaken*, "respecting the elderly." Judaism teaches that as people age, they know more because they have experienced more.

We can benefit from the advice of those who have already gone through the same things we are experiencing. In Judaism, as in other cultures, age and wisdom are related. That is why, in many societies, the wisest people are called the elders (and usually, in fact, they are the oldest). The Torah

הִדּוּר פְּנֵי זָקֵן

respect for the elderly

CAARI (Canadian and American Active Retirees in Israel) believes that life begins at 60. These 60-plus retirees make an annual pilgrimage to affirm their commitment to the Jewish State. The program offers five weeks of volunteer work in schools, hospitals, museums, old age homes, and JNF reforestry.

Israel has a National Insurance Program, which supports Mishenet Zekenim. This Israeli stamp calls attention to this insurance program.

מוֹשַׁב זְקֵנִים

old-age home

The bindery of Lifeline for the Old in Jerusalem. The bindery utilizes the skills of the old to repair old and valued books. The program also repairs the lives of the oldsters.

says: "Rise before the aged and show deference to the old" (Leviticus 19:32).

Dorot

The Hebrew word *dorot* means "generations." It is the name of an organization that devotes its multifaceted efforts to improving the quality of life for weak and isolated Jewish elders in New York City. Dorot has a shop and service escort program in which volunteers shop for, and also escort, elderly people who need a strong arm to get to stores and to medical appointments.

In addition, Dorot has instituted a Shabbat meal program for homebound elders. Here again volunteers deliver kosher meals to the infirm who wish to maintain the Sabbath tradition.

The small but vital and energetic hands-on organization has dedicated its efforts to the mitzvah of respect for the elderly by providing holiday package deliveries, music programs, birthday parties, museum tours, exercise classes, and housing for the homeless. Many of these programs are made possible by high school and college volunteers who provide intergenerational companionship as well as food deliveries.

Caring Jews in hundreds of communities and cities have designed special programs similar to Dorot which mobilize human, physical, and financial resources to perform deeds of tzedakah.

How Old Is Old?

As you get older, your idea of "old" also gets older. Today you may think that a forty-year-old is old, but when you're twenty, sixty is old, and when you're sixty, your definition of old may be eighty-five. The rabbis in the Talmud had their own ideas.

> At sixty one is ready to be an elder, at seventy one is ready for white hairs, at eighty for vigor, at ninety for a bent back, at one hundred it is as if you had died and left the world.
> —Avot 5:21

The Talmud is saying that you weaken physically as you get old. How, then, can we still show respect for the elderly even when they reach a point of mental or physical deterioration?

Throughout history, Jewish communities have made special efforts to care for the elderly in their midst. In the eighteenth and nineteenth centuries, organizations to care for the elderly began to appear. The Mishenet Zekenim ("Support for the Aged") society was founded in Hamburg, Germany, in 1796. This organization made sure that the elderly poor did not starve. Later, Jewish homes for the aged were founded. These were places where elderly persons who could no longer care for themselves could live and be cared for. Generally an institution of this kind was called a moshav zekenim, "home for the aged."

A young child brings joy to an elderly person. Age brings wisdom and love to the young.

Today there are Jewish homes for the aged in many major cities. They are quite different from the ones that existed in the nineteenth century. Many of these facilities have apartments where elderly persons can lived independently. If they want to, the residents can cook for themselves, and for those who do not wish to do so, communal meals are provided. Each community provides programming and medical care. Senior housing also provides transportation for shopping, entertainment, and religious activities. For the frail elderly, there are more traditional nursing homes with round-the-clock nursing care. These facilities also have religious, social, and cultural programs.

Growing Old in America

The population of the United States is growing older. While aging, it is also a healthier population. People live much beyond the sixty-five-year-old retirement age. They follow new pursuits and adventures. Some live in senior housing for convenience. In some cases, nursing homes are a last resort for people who are so frail that their family members can no longer care for them.

The challenge faced by the Jewish community today is how to fulfill the many needs of the aging Jewish population.

Israeli stamp honoring the aged.

**Jewish Community Center
JCC**

**Jewish Vocational Service
JVS**

JFS

Many synagogues and community centers have developed elder-hostel programs. These are one- or two-week retreats covering different topics, ranging from politics to history to film-making. In addition to the courses, there are meals, religious services, and social get-togethers at the elder-hostels.

Retirees as Resources

In Judaism, as in many other traditions, an older person is viewed as having much to offer. With age comes experience, and this is an important form of wisdom. For this reason age has often been equated with knowledge. As we read in Proverbs 20:29, "The glory of the young is their strength, the glory of the old is the hoary head [white hair]."

The knowledge older people have provides them with an opportunity to perform the mitzvot of helping and teaching others. Formally this is done through mentoring programs. A mentor is a person who knows a lot about a particular subject and advises another person in the same field. Sometimes the mentor just listens to what is going on. At other times the mentor will offer help in solving a business problem.

The Jewish community has established many mentor programs. Synagogues and community centers look to seniors as a major source of volunteers. Among other things, volunteers answer phones, tutor, and provide business help or advice.

Jewish Vocational Services (JVS) offices offer retired people the opportunity to volunteer as mentors. Through JVS they can network with others who have a great deal of experience. Mentors provide advice on how and where to look for work; they may even have contacts who will help job-seekers. Sometimes mentors volunteer in an actual business, acting as consultants.

Finally, Jewish community centers, Jewish Family Services, and Jewish homes for the aged offer many options for families that have frail elderly members—persons who need constant care because their health is deteriorating. When family members are unable to provide round-the-clock attention, they can bring their frail elderly to adult care centers for a few hours of socialization and activities during the day. In addition, visiting nurses stop by the house and make sure the elderly person is taking his or her medication. Meals on wheels programs make sure that those who are too weak to cook or shop have food every day. There are Jewish homes for the aged that provide all this and more, twenty-four hours a day.

Seniors and Sensitivity
An insight into aging is found in the Talmud (Shabbat 152a). The great sage Rabbi Yehudah ha-Nasi (known simply as Rabbi) met the sage Rabbi Shimon ben Halafta after not having seen him for quite some time. Rabbi asked: "Why did we not welcome you on the festivals, as my ancestors received yours?" Rabbi Shimon ben Halafta responded: "The rocks have grown tall, the near has become distant, and two have become three." His curious answer meant that the rocks seemed higher, and whatever had once seemed near now seemed farther away, because it was difficult to travel at his age. "Two have become three" meant that instead of walking on two legs, he now had to use a cane.

There is much we can learn from this conversation. What could Rabbi have done in advance to help Shimon ben Halafta? What can we learn from Shimon's response that would help us make the Jewish community at more inviting place for the elderly? As the Bible tells us, "Do not abandon me in my old age" (Psalms 71:9).

Honor Your Father and Your Mother
There can be no *shlom bayit* if there is no *kebud av v'em*, "honor for your father and mother." Jewish tradition teaches that you must honor your father and your mother in the same manner as you revere God.

A happy Jewish home means *shlom bayit*: it means a center of love and cooperation; it means a home in which you drink in ideas and ethics, which will mold your thinking, your attitudes and your actions; it means a place where the Fifth Commandment, "honor your father and your mother" is always obeyed. The Talmud also says that it means a home where parents love their children and treat them with gentleness and respect.

Teachings from Tradition

There is wisdom in the aged, and understanding in those of long life.

<Job12:12>

As people age, their opinions change.

<Shabbat 142a>

Any nation that has no elderly deserves to be destroyed.

<Alphabet of Ben Sira>

Do not shame	אַל תְּבַיֵּשׁ
the old,	אֱנוֹשׁ יָשִׁישׁ
for we shall all	כִּי נִמָּנֶה
be old.	מִזְקֵנִים

<Ben Sira 8:6>

בִּקוּר חוֹלִים

Bikkur Holim:
Visiting the Sick

Once upon a time, there was a disease called smallpox. As it spread around the world, millions of people contracted it, and vast numbers of them died. In 1967 the World Health Organization of the United Nations began a worldwide campaign to vaccinate people against smallpox. The results were incredible. From an average of 10 to 15 million cases a year, the numbers got lower and lower. By 1979 there were no reported cases of smallpox in the world. Today, smallpox exists only in a vial, kept under high security at the Centers for Disease Control in Atlanta, Georgia.

The fight against smallpox is one of the many triumphs of medicine over disease. Diseases spread in many ways, some by breathing, some by direct contact. In the modern world, diseases can traverse the earth very rapidly. A common flu can make its way around the world in six weeks. It is no wonder that people often shun someone who becomes ill, especially if the disease is unknown.

What are you like when you are sick? Do you want to be left alone? Do you get bored after a few days? Often, you wish that someone would be with you and talk to you. The presence of another person helps you forget about your illness, and your loneliness. A visit lets you know that people remember you, and miss you, just as you miss them.

World Health Organization
WHO

בִּקוּר חוֹלִים
visiting the sick

The Mitzvah of Bikkur Holim

Visiting a person who is ill is one of the most important mitzvot. It is so important, according to Rabbi Akiva, that "a person who does not visit the sick is like a shedder of blood," because failing to visit makes the sick person even sicker through loneliness and sadness. In all probability, *bikkur holim,* "visiting the sick," is considered so important because our natural reaction is to stay away from a person who is ill. We don't want to catch what they have!

The mitzvah of bikkur holim forces us to forget our own fears and selfish reactions. We are to place the ill person, who is in need, above our personal concerns. We are to make every effort to visit the ill.

Some people are reluctant to visit the sick because they do not know how to act around someone who is ill. There is a very easy solution for this. Think of what you would want people to do for you if you were ill. Then do those things for your friend who is sick.

Here are some guidelines. Don't dwell on the person's illness—unless that is what he or she wants to talk about. Don't bring bad news to a person who is sick. You will find that just your presence makes a difference. While a sick person will certainly appreciate any gift you bring, the effort you make in visiting is enough to show that you care.

The Children of Chernobyl

In 1986, the Chernobyl nuclear power plant exploded, and the Ukraine was flooded with radiation—ninety times the amount unleashed by the atomic bomb dropped on Hiroshima. Today 850,000 Ukrainian children breathe poisoned air, drink radioactive milk and water, and eat food grown in contaminated earth.

The Children of Chernobyl project, a Habad organization, has brought fifteen hundred of these children to Israel, where they are cared for by physicians and volunteers. Within a year, with proper nutrition and medical treatment, most of the children begin to recover.

Even now, thousands of Jewish children remain on the waiting list for treatment.

A group of children rescued by the dedicated supporters of Habad's Children of Chernobyl. This is the 22nd rescue mission.

Hospitals and Hospitality

Most people are very uncomfortable when it comes to paying a sick call. You wonder: When is it all right to visit? What should I say? How should I act? How long should I stay? The answers to these questions are provided by Jewish traditional sources. Since bikkur holim is such an important mitzvah, they advise us on how to perform it.

Here are some helpful hints on visiting the sick:

1. If the ill person is related to you, visit as soon as possible. If you do not know the person that well, wait three days. Visit as often as possible, as long as you do not tire the sick person. When you visit, don't come too early or too late in the day, and don't stay too long.

2. Do not be at a higher level than the patient. If the person is in bed, it is okay to sit on a chair.

3. An important reason to visit a sick person is to find out what he or she needs. Also, say a prayer for a person who is sick.

4. Be cheerful when visiting. Use your judgment when talking to someone who is ill. Don't give the person false hopes, but don't be discouraging either. Encourage the sick person to talk.

5. Don't visit someone who is so sick that socialization would be difficult. Instead, pray for the sick person, and do what you can to help, such as by finding out if he or she needs anything that you can provide.

The best advice for fulfilling the mitzvah of bikkur holim is to think back to a time when you were sick. What could someone have done to make you feel better? Use your experience to help someone else on the way to a *refuah shelemah*, a complete recovery.

A Formal Invitation

Bikkur holim is such a crucial mitzvah that there are formal organizations to provide this service. These are called bikkur holim societies. Often, they are associated with a synagogue. The volunteers from the synagogue go to hospitals and nursing homes, or visit shut-ins on a regular basis. Sometimes they know the people they are visiting, but they may also be complete strangers. It doesn't matter.

רְפוּאָה שְׁלֵמָה

a complete recovery

This *refuah shelemah* booklet is called "Fountain of Life". It contains prayers and thoughts for a complete recovery. This booklet is usually presented by Bikur Holim societies or hospital chaplains to Jewish patients.

חַלּוֹת

hallot

Israeli stamp promoting health insurance

Israeli stamp promoting health insurance

Many synagogue bikkur holim societies make it a point to visit people before Shabbat and holidays. In this way they include the sick in their Shabbat or holiday celebration. Often, they will bring small challot or other holiday-related items as gifts. Perhaps one person will bring a guitar and sing songs. The volunteer, or a visiting rabbi, may say a prayer with the patient. All these activities show the person who is ill that he or she is not forgotten in the Jewish community.

If you are ever in a big city, and you drive by a hospital on a Friday afternoon, there is a very good chance you will see a school bus or van parked outside the hospital. The words "bikkur holim society" will be emblazoned on the outside of the bus. The members of the society are volunteers who go from hospital to hospital, fulfilling this important mitzvah.

Health Insurance and Jewish History

Because the mitzvah of bikkur holim is so important, it is not surprising that Jewish communities made it a communal responsibility. Historically, bikkur holim societies were different from the present-day variety. In earlier centuries, the role of these associations was to provide actual medical care for the sick.

The first record of such an organization is in Spain, in 1336, where a shoemakers' guild in Saragossa provided its members with sick care. This type of association slowly spread to European Jewish communities, as Spanish Jews fled the Inquisition and settled elsewhere.

By the eighteenth century, there were bikkur holim societies throughout Europe. They provided a type of health insurance. A person who was a member was entitled to medical care when ill. You could become a member through your professional guild or association. The poor were not overlooked. There were special bikkur holim societies to provide for their medical needs. At times, a communal tax was imposed to make sure that the societies could function. The care provided included doctors, midwives, surgeons, and druggists.

In some communities, the bikkur holim society was very influential. While members of the Jewish community were obligated to pay taxes for the communal good, the bikkur holim society saw to it that doctors were not taxed—as long as they treated the poor for free.

The bikkur holim associations also provided volunteers to visit the sick and make sure that no patient was lonely. It is this activity that modern bikkur holim societies still carry out today.

Do Not Enter

As important as visiting the sick may be, there are concerns that people have. Some diseases are highly contagious. How would bikkur holim be carried out in Zaire, where the deadly Ebola virus killed hundreds in the spring of 1995? What should you do if doctors warn you to stay away from people who are ill, yet the mitzvah of bikkur holim commands you to be with them? What do you do if a person is in quarantine? How do you fulfill the mitzvah of bikkur holim? This is a question that many people asked in the early days of the AIDS epidemic, before we knew exactly how it was transmitted. It will probably arise in the future, as some new "super-bug" develops and spreads.

Bubonic Plague and Prejudice

One of the most feared diseases to strike humanity was the bubonic plague. It swept through Europe in 1348–50, killing between a quarter and half of the population. People panicked, attempting to flee as rumors of the oncoming plague spread. The disease itself, known as the Black Death, spread quickly and lethally.

The Jewish community was doubly affected. People throughout Europe looked for the source of this disease. Was it divine punishment? Was it an evil plot? As at other times in the fourteenth century, the Jews were seen to be the culprits. Jewish communities were accused of poisoning the wells of their neighbors. In 1348, at a castle on Lake Geneva, a number of Jews were tortured into confessing that they indeed had poisoned wells.

These "confessions" were sent to many cities in Germany, resulting in panic and reprisals against Jews. In a few places the rulers spoke out on behalf of their Jewish residents. Pope Clement VI issued a papal bull defending the Jews. But the panic had become widespread. Jews were expelled from many cities and towns. As the panic became overwhelming, more

מַגֵּפָה

Plague

Black Death

A 14th century French painting depicting a Black Death burial scene. Note the bodies wrapped in white shrouds.

מִי שֶׁבֵּרַךְ

**a prayer often recited
on behalf of
a sick person**

Jews were tortured into confessing a plot to destroy Christian Europe. Thousands of Jews were massacred by the terror-stricken populace. Thus, Jews in Europe not only fell victim to the bubonic plague, but to the terror and hostility the plague left among its survivors.

The aftershocks of the Black Death have been felt even in modern times. Long before the plague, Jews had been victims of hatred, but the plague led to the stereotype of the devious Jew conspiring to destroy the world. In the twentieth century many outbreaks of anti-Semitism have been stirred up by this idea.

Contagious Diseases

Patients who are highly infectious are quarantined. Visitors must wear masks, gowns, and gloves, and must wash themselves thoroughly after leaving the presence of the patient. In this way, the disease is not transmitted to others.

When a patient is highly contagious, visiting is restricted. The procedures just described are followed by doctors and nurses, and also by rabbis fulfilling the mitzvah of bikkur holim with someone who is very ill. Chances are, the hospital would not allow other visitors, even from a bikkur holim society, in such cases. Even if you cannot visit someone who is ill, there are things you can do, such as sending a card or phoning. A very important act is to offer a prayer on the sick person's behalf. This can be done formally at a service, with the prayer called Mi Sheberach, "The One Who Blesses." It can also be done informally, by making up your own prayer. Try to let the ill person know that you have prayed for his or her recovery; it will provide a source of hope.

Teachings from Tradition

One who visits a sick person lessens that person's illness by one-sixtieth.

<Nedarim 39b>

One who visits the sick causes that person to live, and one who does not visit the sick causes that person to die.

<Nedarim 40a>

Grant us a perfect healing to all our wounds, for You are a faithful and merciful God, Ruler and Healer. We praise You Adonai, our God, Healer of the sick.

<Siddur>

Do not tarry   אַל תְּאַחֵר

to visit the sick.   לְבַקֵּר אִישׁ חוֹלֶה.

<Talmud>

חֶסֶד שֶׁל אֱמֶת

Hesed shel Emet:
Respect for the Dead

חֶסֶד שֶׁל אֱמֶת

respect for the dead

Have you ever wandered through the ancient Egypt exhibit at a museum? The treasures taken from Egyptian pyramids are fascinating. Everything found in pyramids was meant to be used by the dead pharaoh in the afterlife. Today, many dead pharaohs are spending eternity as exhibits in museums for our enjoyment.

Egypt's rulers weren't the only ones who gave a lot of attention to preparing for the unknown. All societies have rituals that provide a way of saying a final goodbye to a loved one. Some are quite simple, others as elaborate as the burial of an Egyptian pharaoh.

In Jewish tradition, many different acts are involved in the preparations for funeral and burial. These mitzvot are concerned with the honor and respect we are to show those who have died. They are called *hesed shel emet*, a Hebrew term meaning a "true act of kindness." It refers to any mitzvah related to the burial of an individual.

Why are the mitzvot connected with burial considered true acts of kindness? With all other mitzvot, our motives may be selfish rather than altruistic. There is always the possibility that the person performing the mitzvah may get a benefit in return from the recipient. But there is no way a dead person can repay you. Therefore, mitzvot performed for a dead person are considered to have no selfish motive.

74 •

There is another reason that hesed shel emet is considered a tremendous mitzvah. Most people are afraid of anything having to do with death. Overcoming this fear, and showing honor to the dead, takes on great significance.

Respect for the Dead

Jewish tradition provides much guidance regarding the treatment of the dead. According to the Torah, burial is to take place on the same day, before the sun sets (Deuteronomy 21:23). By talmudic times, a different point of view was presented. What if the funeral plans can't be made immediately, if a coffin has to be brought in, or people from another town need to be informed? The Talmud permits a short delay if the intention is to honor the dead (Sanhedrin 46b–47a). Today, short delays are permitted so that family members who live in distant places can make it to the funeral.

The Talmud looks at other issues of respect for those who have died. A person who comes across an unidentified body is obligated to bury it at that spot (Semahot 4). Respect for the dead is of such overriding importance that other important mitzvot may be delayed to fulfill it. For example, the Talmud says that Torah study may be interrupted in order to participate in a funeral procession (Ketubbot 17a).

The mitzvot relating to the dead are unique for an important but obvious reason. They are acts of gemilut hasadim (lovingkindness) that cannot be repaid. When one performs a mitzvah out of respect for the dead, it is solely for the purpose of honoring the dead, whether it was a family member, a friend, or a complete stranger.

The Mitzvah of Hesed shel Emet

When a Jew dies, the corpse is prepared for burial through a series of rituals. Even though the soul is no longer with the person's body, the body must still be treated with respect, and the rituals ensure this. The body must be kept company at all times. This is called *shemirah*, guarding. Those doing the guarding recite psalms as they sit with the body. The preparation of the body for burial is called *taharah*, purification. The body is washed and traditionally dressed in a white shroud. After this, it is placed in a simple wooden coffin. Throughout

מֵת
a dead person

שְׁמִירָה
guarding

טַהֲרָה
purification

• 75

חֶבְרָא קַדִּישָׁא

Holy Society

Leaders of the Prague Jewish community at the grave of Rabbi Judah Loew.

the entire process, the deceased is never alone. Men prepare male corpses for burial, and women prepare female ones.

The people who prepare a body for burial are members of an organization called *hevra kadisha*, an Aramaic term meaning "holy society." This is not a professional organization; any Jew can join a hevra kadisha and be trained in the mitzvot of hesed shel emet.

Hevra kadisha societies have been around for a long time. They go back as far as the fourteenth century in Spain and Germany.

Setting the Rules

One of the earliest records of a hevra kadisha society is from sixteenth-century Prague. By the seventeenth century it had set regulations regarding burial fees, graves, and rules for erecting tombstones. What makes this particular society interesting is that we know who established the rules. It was a rabbi named Judah Loew ben Bezalel (1525–1609), known by the title MaHaRaL. In addition to being a rabbi, he was mathematician and philosopher.

Though he was influential in many different fields, today MaHaRaL is remembered for one thing in particular. There is a legend that grew around him about the golem of Prague. According to the legend, the MaHaRaL created a human-like being out of earth in order to protect the Jews of Prague in times of need. This creature came to life when God's name was placed on its forehead. It then fulfilled the tasks that the rabbi set for it. Today, many Jews know this story (it has even been filmed!), but few know that the real MaHaRal of Prague established the rules that have guided hevra kadisha societies for centuries.

Originally, hevra kadisha societies were set up to bury only the members of the association. Being a member of a hevra kadisha was considered a great honor for which people competed. It was a totally voluntary position. Among the well-known members of hevra kadisha organizations were the British philanthropist, Sir Moses Montefiore, and the young Shneur Zalman, who later went on the found the Lubavitcher Hasidic movement.

Today, these groups provide this service to any Jew. Every

Jewish community has at least one hevra kadisha. While in the past, these society were associated with Orthodox synagogues, more and more Conservative and Reform synagogues are establishing a hevra kadisha to provide their members with the opportunity to perform hesed shel emet.

There is one traditional role that the hevra kadisha no longer provides. It used to be responsible for the cemetery. People would buy a burial plot through a hevra kadisha. The hevra kadisha would not only perform the burial but would make sure that the plots were taken care of on a regular basis. Today, most cemeteries are privately owned and hire workers to maintain the land. The few synagogues that still own their own cemeteries may indeed have a hevra kadisha whose members will spend a Sunday afternoon mowing the grass and making sure the paths are clean and the tombstones are in proper shape.

A Few Good Menschen

The mitzvah of hesed shel emet can be emotionally difficult to perform under normal circumstances. Israel has volunteers who carry out the mitzvah of hesed shel emet in wartime. Israel prides itself on the treatment of its war casualties. Many Jews who do not serve in the armed forces for religious reasons, or are too old for army duty, have volunteered for this special hevra kadisha.

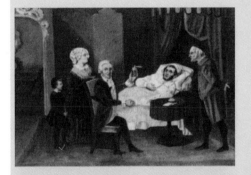

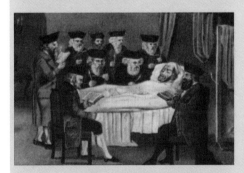

In times of catastrophe, it becomes even harder to fulfill hesed shel emet. If you have ever seen a news report of a terrorist bombing in Israel, you will have seen medical workers, police, and soldiers at the scene. You may also have seen a number of Orthodox Jews with stretchers at the scene. While some of them are likely to be medical workers, many are from a very special hevra kadisha. They have taken on the mitzvah of helping to bury victims of terror. It is the nature of the victims' death that makes this type of hesed shel emet so difficult to carry out. These hevra kadisha groups must deal with bodies that met a gruesome, violent end. They have to deal with many corpses at once, and often they must literally gather pieces of flesh for burial. It is an emotionally troubling task, yet people volunteer for it because respect for the dead is of such importance in Jewish tradition.

These three paintings show the Prague hevra kadisha performing their duties; reciting Psalms at a deathbed and transferring the body for burial.

You do not have to belong to a hevra kadisha to fulfill the

שִׁבְעָה

week of mourning

מַצֵּבָה

tombstone

כֹּהֵן

kohen

פ"נ

פֹּה נִקְבַּר

here is buried

תנצב"ה

May his/her soul be bound
in bonds of
everlasting life.

תְּהֵא נִשְׁמָתוֹ/נִשְׁמָתָה
צְרוּרָה בִּצְרוֹר הַחַיִּים.

mitzvah of hesed shel emet. There are other ways to do this mitzvah. Everyone who attends a burial can take part in burying the deceased by putting a shovelful of earth into the grave. This is considered the last loving act a person can do to show respect for the deceased.

Other mitzvot include making a donation in memory of the deceased person. Comforting mourners is also a mitzvah. This is done by going to the mourners' home during shiva, the weeklong period of mourning. You can be part of a minyan that holds a service at the mourners' house during shiva. You can visit the people who are in mourning. If you don't know what to say to comfort them, that's okay. It is most important that those who are in mourning see that others care enough to spend some time with them.

Written in Stone

When you visit a Jewish cemetery, the tombstones tell a story. Of course, each stone contains information about the individual buried beneath it. In addition, there is information on Jewish tombstones that you will not find in other cemeteries.

Some tombstones have a carving of two hands held close together to form a triangle. Each hand is held open between the middle and ring finger. This is the sign of the priestly blessing. When you see this carved on a tombstone, it means that the person buried there is a kohen.

Another tombstone may have a water jug carved on it. This is a symbol of the levites, whose ancient function was to wash the hands of the kohen in preparation for his priestly duty. When you see the water jug on a tombstone, you known that the person buried there was a levite.

In some cemeteries there are tombstones shaped like tree stumps. These were erected for people who died young, either as children or in their teens. The stump represents the tree of life which was cut down too soon.

There are also Hebrew letters on tombstones. The letters פ"נ are an abbreviation for *poh nikbar*, "here lies buried"; תנצב"ה stand for the words תְּהֵא נִשְׁמָתוֹ/נִשְׁמָתָה צְרוּרָה בִּצְרוֹר הַחַיִּים, "may his/her soul be bound in the bonds of everlasting life," the Jewish equivalent of "rest in peace."

78 •

Potter's Field

In Western society, special cemeteries are set aside for people who are too poor to afford a grave, people who die and cannot be identified, and criminals. These cemeteries are referred to as a "potter's field," an expression that comes from the book of Matthew in the Christian New Testament.

In Judaism there is no such concept. Everybody is considered equal in death. No one is to have a more elaborate coffin than anybody else. Yet there are cases where people die and no family members are left to bury them. This can happen when a person has lived a very long life, outliving all friends and relatives. In such cases, a synagogue or hevra kadisha will take on the responsibility of burying the person, treating the body exactly as they would treat any other. There are even individuals who set aside tzedakah to be used specifically in such cases. In this symbolic way, no Jew is ever alone in death.

There is one final way to fulfill the mitzvah of hesed shel emet. Every Jew who has died should be remembered regularly through the recitation of Kaddish and attendance at Yizkor memorial services. Some people take on this responsibility for deceased persons who have no one to remember them. They see this as an especially important mitzvah after the Holocaust. So many millions of Jews died without proper burial, and with no one to say Kaddish for them, that every Jew today is obligated to take on this form of hesed shel emet.

Special Exhibits

In 1995 there was a tremendous controversy in Israel. Someone had put out a catalogue selling items from the Holocaust, including soap and lampshades said to have been made from the skin of human victims. There was a tremendous uproar that this was extremely disrespectful toward the victims of the Holocaust. Eventually, these items were withdrawn from sale.

With Holocaust museums and exhibits being displayed in more and more places, issues of hesed shel emet have arisen. These exhibits are important ways of making sure people do not forget the tragedy of the Holocaust. Yet there are concerns that even displaying photographs from concentration camps is disrespectful to the people who were murdered there. Do

you think it is possible to fulfill the commandment to remember the Holocaust and, at the same time, observe the mitzvah of hesed shel emet?

With regard to museums, let's go back to those fantastic exhibits of Egyptian mummies. Do you think it is okay to display mummies as museum objects, or is it a violation of hesed shel emet, showing disrespect for persons who have long been dead?

Teachings from Tradition

The whole community knew that Aaron had breathed his last. The entire house of Israel mourned Aaron for thirty days.

<Numbers 20:29>

The dust returns to the ground as it was, and the spirit returns to Adonai who gave it.

<Kohelet 12:7>

One may interrupt the study of Torah to take part in a funeral.

<Ket. 17a>

There is a season for everything,　לַכֹּל זְמָן

a time for　וְעֵת

every experience　לְכָל־חֵפֶץ

under heaven.　תַּחַת הַשָּׁמַיִם:

A time for being born,　עֵת לָלֶדֶת

and a time for dying.　וְעֵת לָמוּת . . .

<Kohelet 3:1–2>

בַּל תַּשְׁחִית

Bal Tashhit:
Do Not Destroy

On the night of March 24, 1989, the oil tanker *Exxon Valdez* hit a reef in Prince William Sound, Alaska. When the ship ran aground on the reef it began to leak oil, and continued to leak oil for two days.

Many tankers were sent to the area, and the oil still left on the *Exxon Valdez* was transferred to those ships. The Coast Guard began cleaning and containment efforts. Thousands of volunteers washed the oil from the stones on the beaches. By the time it was over, more than one thousand miles of the Alaskan coast had been coated with oil, killing thousands of animals, including sea otters and birds.

That early spring night in Alaska was the beginning of the largest oil spill in U.S. history. Since the 1960s, scientists have been working on ways to deal with oil spills. The most common solution is to do what the Coast Guard did in Alaska: "vacuum" the oil off the water. There are more unusual and creative solutions as well.

In the late 1970s a group of Israeli scientists announced one such alternative. They had discovered a biological solution to the growing number of oil spills. They were experimenting with different types of micro-organisms that loved to snack on oil. Biology provides part of the answer to water problems. Part of the process used in treatment plants is to

Israeli stamp honoring the environment

"clean" the waste water we produce with bacteria which change the waste to a more environment-friendly type of sludge.

Oil slicks aren't the only problem. In the 1980s and 1990s, many beaches along the New York and New Jersey shore were closed for weeks in the hot summer months. Garbage dumped into the water was making its way to shore. This garbage included biological waste from hospitals and medical offices. People swimming in the water might accidentally swallow water that contained a great deal of dangerous bacteria. Someone walking along the beach could step on a syringe.

The Mitzvah of Bal Tashhit

How would you feel if you couldn't go to the beach on a hot summer day? What would you do if you were told your water wasn't safe to drink? These are growing problems being faced throughout the world. The problem arises from our use of the world and its resources. The question is: when does use become abuse?

In Judaism, there is a mitzvah that defines how we can use nature. This is the mitzvah of *bal tashhit*, a Hebrew term meaning "do not destroy." It is based on a commandment given in the Torah. The commandment tells us that when there is a war, and a city is under siege, the soldiers may eat from the trees around the city, but they are not allowed to chop them down. In this way, the trees will be there to provide food for years to come.

The Torah also presents other ideas regarding our relationship with nature. In the story of creation, God tells humanity that we are guardians of the world. We are allowed to use nature, but God also commands us to tend it and take care of it.

If a Tree Falls in a Forest . . .

Concern for nature is an integral part of Jewish tradition and takes on many forms. In Pirke de Rabbi Eliezer (chap. 34) one point of view is presented: When a fruit-bearing tree is cut down, its groans go from one end of the world to the other, yet no sound is heard. This teaches us that trees are considered life.

בַּל תַּשְׁחִית
do not destroy

Slowly but surely, the Land of Israel is being reforested. This is the Maccabee forest in Modin.

Carefully the youngsters cover the fragile roots of the saplings. In years to come the wastelands of Israel will burst into foliage with millions of green budding trees.

Society for the Protection of Nature SPN

Society for the Preservation of Nature stamps.

A different perspective comes from a commentary on the story of creation. Genesis 1:26 says, "And God said, Let us make humanity in our own image, according to our likeness, and they shall rule over the fish in the sea and the birds in the sky and the cattle and all the earth, and all the creeping things that creep on the earth."

The commentator Nachmanides (1194–1270), known in Hebrew as Ramban, wondered what was meant by "all the earth." He explained it as meaning that humanity "shall rule over the land itself, to uproot and pull down." He was also intrigued by Genesis 1:28, which says that humanity will master the earth. Ramban explained this as meaning that "God gave them the power to do as they wish with all the cattle and the reptiles and all that creeps in the dust." In other words, people are the masters of the earth.

Here are two different perspectives from Jewish tradition, one concerned with the earth and what lives upon it, the other saying that we are masters of the earth. Can they complement each other and fulfill the mitzvah of bal tashhit?

Trees of Life

The Torah is called the tree of life because it teaches us how to make our lives better. An important way of doing this is through the mitzvot that remind us about our responsibility to nature.

As with other mitzvot, organizations have been founded to help fulfill ecological mitzvot. Anyone who attends religious school is familiar with the blue-and-white boxes of the Jewish National Fund. The tzedakah collected by the JNF is used to plant trees in Israel. In close to a century of existence, the JNF has planted entire forests. As the trees grow, they provide homes for many animals, and a cool retreat from the hot Middle Eastern sun.

Another organization is the Society for the Protection of Nature in Israel. It tries to make sure that the numerous environments in Israel are not damaged by unnecessary building. Of special concern is the desert, which contains many unusual forms of animal life. The society is also well known for its guided tours of Israel. Instead of visiting the usual tourist sites, these tours are meant to heighten your appreciation for the natural beauty of Israel. They take you hiking in the Galilee or camping in the Negev.

Caring for the Environment

The Jewish National Fund is probably the best-known group concerned with environmental issues in Israel. Known in Hebrew as *Keren Kayemet le-Yisrael,* it was established in 1901 by the Zionist Organization. Its original purpose was to raise money and purchase land in the historic Jewish homeland, Israel.

After Israel gained its independence in 1948, the JNF took on a new mission which it still holds today. Now the JNF concentrates on land improvement and development. It was instrumental in draining swamps in order to create farmland in the Jezreel and Huleh valleys.

The Jewish National Fund's best-known task is afforestation, planting trees. Through the JNF, Jews around the world help plant trees in the land of Israel. These young forests are used for recreational purposes. At certain times of the year, such as Tu BiShevat, Israeli students help with the planting of young saplings, some of which were purchased through donations by other students around the world. Trees are planted to commemorate various occasions: births, anniversaries, a Bar or Bat Mitzvah or graduation. Sad occasions are remembered as well as happy ones. After the assassination of Israeli Prime Minister Yitzhak Rabin in November 1995, Hebrew school students around the world donated money to plant thousands of trees in the newly established Yitzhak Rabin Forest.

In the United States, there are also Jewish organizations concerned with protecting the environment. One of them is Shomrei Adamah, Guardians of the Earth. It tries to make all Jews aware of the mitzvah of bal tashhit. Another organization linking Judaism to environmental responsibility is the Coalition on the Environment and Jewish Life (COEJL). It is an umbrella organization for various Jewish groups dealing with environmental issues. Its member organizations include Jewish women's groups, Jewish War Veterans, the various religious denominations, and educational groups. COEJL urges people to act politically on behalf of the environment, such as by protecting the ancient forests of North America.

קֶרֶן קַיֶּמֶת לְיִשְׂרָאֵל
Jewish National Fund
JNF

שׁוֹמְרֵי אֲדָמָה
Guardians of the Earth

Coalition on the Environment and Jewish Life
COEJL

Jewish War Veterans
JWV

טוּ בִּשְׁבָט
New Year of the Tree

First fruits blossom on a fig tree. The Talmud says: "When one sees a fig tree one should make a blessing, thanking God for creating it."

All these organizations have created programs to be used in schools and synagogues to teach about this commandment. Shomrei Adamah, COEJL, and the Jewish National Fund have developed ways to make us aware of the environment through Jewish holidays. There are Haggadot for Tu BiShevat, the New Year of the Trees, that remind us just how important trees and plants are to our survival. Many stories in the Bible are given a new emphasis. The Garden of Eden is viewed as the ideal relationship we should try to have with nature. The story of Noah is taken to be a warning about ecological disaster.

The efforts of these organizations are meant to remind us that God made us guardians of the world. As guardians we can use it, but we must also protect it. The mitzvah of bal tashhit is the Jewish way of finding a balance with nature—using it for our pleasure, but making sure God's creation will be there for future generations.

Why Tu Bi Shevat?

Why is Tu Bi Shevat increasingly looked upon as an ecological holiday? Tu BiShevat, the fifteenth day of the month of Shevat, was a time in ancient Israel when the tax on fruit was due. Though a minor holiday, this New Year of the Trees was kept when the Jews were exiled from ancient Israel. Its new meaning no longer involved the tree-tax, but stressed trees, specifically the trees of Israel. An elaborate Seder eventually developed, and gave centuries of Diaspora Jews a means of relating to Israel through its produce.

In modern times, TuBiShevat is the traditional time when schools collect money which the JNF uses to plant trees in Israel. Many temples also hold Tu BiShevat Seders where fruits specific to the land of Israel (figs, carobs) are eaten. In these ways, Jews outside of Israel still use Tu BiShevat as a way to connect with the land of Israel.

In the United States, an additional meaning has been given to Tu BiShevat. It is a holiday that raises our ecological awareness. Ecology ties in to Tu BiShevat because of the focus on trees. While we often take nature for granted, Tu BiShevat stresses the importance of nature. Because nature, and what it gives us, is the focal point of this holiday, we concentrate on texts and mitzvot having to do with nature and our role in nature. In this way Tu Bi Shevat is the ideal vehicle for teaching about the mitzvot of ecology.

Finding a Balance

We tend to think of ecological issues as modern concerns, but the problems we face today have been faced by humanity before. The issue of pollution is discussed in traditional Jewish texts. The Talmud treats such issues as air, water, and noise pollution.

For example, a permanent threshing floor for threshing grain must be a distance of 50 cubits from a city. Out of concern for the effect it will have on other foodstuffs, it must also be at least 50 cubits from a neighbor's fields and produce so as not to do damage (Bava Batra 24b). The same talmudic tractate also says that certain types of buildings and businesses must be kept away from water sources, while other businesses must be 50 cubits outside of a city because of the stench they produce (Bava Batra 18a–b, 25a). In addition, If you are going to set up a business that will be excessively noisy, you must get permission from your neighbors first (Bava Batra 20b–21a).

The land for the first settlements in Palestine was purchased by Keren Kayemet le-Yisrael (Jewish National Fund), established in 1901 as the land-purchasing agency of the Zionist movement.
The Jewish National Fund depended on small sums of money collected from Jews throughout the world. The blue-and-white JNF box found a place in millions of Jewish homes.

Tree planting in Israel.

Teachings from Tradition

When in your war against a city you have to besiege it for a long time in order to capture it, you must not destroy its trees. You may eat of them, but you must not chop them down.

<Devarim 20:19>

It is forbidden to live in a town that does not have a garden.

<Yerushalmi, Kiddushin 4:12>

When God created the first human, God showed the human all the trees in the Garden of Eden. God said to the human: "See my works, how beautiful and how praiseworthy they are. Everything I have created I have done for your sake. Think of this and do not pollute or destroy My world. If you pollute it, there will be no one to fix it after you.

<Kohelet Rabbah 7:13>

How numerous are Your works, Adonai. You have made them all in wisdom, the earth is full of Your creations.

<Siddur>

Trees	כָּל הָאִילָנוֹת
for man's companionship	לַהֲנָאָתָן שֶׁל הַבְּרִיּוֹת
were created	נִבְרָאוּ

<Genesis Rabbah.>

צַעַר בַּעֲלֵי חַיִּים

Tsa'ar Ba'alei Hayyim:
Cruelty to Animals

When you are sick you take some medicine. When you are hungry you eat a hamburger. In all probability you have shoes, a belt, or a bag made of leather. We couldn't use these things unless we used animals. Animals are an important source of food and many other products in our lives. Medicines are tested on animals to determine whether they are safe for humans. New foods and cosmetics are tested on animals as well. We use organs from animals to help save human lives. Experiments and studies of all kinds are carried out on white mice and laboratory rats. Is such research right? Is it fair to the animals? Is it fair to people?

The Hamster That Made Aliyah
In 1930, a researcher at Hebrew University in Jerusalem was busily trying to find a cure for a tropical disease. Like many medical researchers, he was experimenting with rodents. Instead of mice or rats, he was using Chinese hamsters. The only problem was that they would not breed. Whenever the scientist needed more animals, he had to order them from China.

Another Hebrew University scientist, a zoologist, was going on a trip to Syria and said he would bring back some hamsters from there. The zoologist kept his promise, bringing back some hamsters to be used for medical research. He also brought back a different type of hamster, a golden hamster.

The zoologist wanted to keep the golden hamsters as pets, but they kept escaping from their cage, so he gave them to Hebrew University's research laboratory. After a few months, there were a number of baby hamsters. In fact, the Syrian golden hamsters became so accustomed to their new home that pretty soon the laboratory had too many hamsters.

The hamsters were shipped to other laboratories all over the world. Eventually, they also had too many hamsters. Scientists began to take the animals home as pets for their children. Then pet dealers discovered the golden hamster. Because of their journey from Syria to Jerusalem, hamsters are now one of the most popular pets in the world today.

The Mitzvah of Avoiding Tsa'ar Ba'alei Hayyim

The story of the golden hamster is both a happy and a sad one. Anyone who has had a pet knows the joy of caring for an animal. We should not forget that these creatures were first brought to Hebrew University to be used in medical experiments. The experiment was to help humanity by finding a cure to a disease. But some of the animals used in the lab would have to die in the process.

There is yet another mitzvah meant to make us aware of the world around us. This commandments relates specifically to animals. In Hebrew it is called *tsa'ar ba'alei hayyim*, literally, "the pain of living creatures." This mitzvah reminds us of the importance of animal life and commands us to avoid being cruel to animals.

The Torah includes many mitzvot dealing with animals. In ancient Israel, farmers plowing a field were instructed in the Torah (Deuteronomy 22:10) not to harness an ox and a donkey together. These animals are not equally strong, and it would be unfair to match them with each other. Imagine a football game between a fifth-grade class and high school football team. While both groups can play the same game, the high school team is bigger, stronger, and could even harm the younger players. These two teams would never play each other, for the same reason that an ox and a donkey could not plow together.

צַעַר בַּעֲלֵי חַיִּים

cruelty to animals

Three chapters later (Deuteronomy 25:4), there is yet another instruction. An animal working in a field cannot be muzzled. It must be free to eat whatever it wants while working.

We are permitted to use animals in other ways as well. We are allowed to eat them. An example given in the Torah, in Deuteronomy 22:6, is that of a person coming across a bird's nest. Taking the eggs is permitted, but the mother bird is sent away first. Why do you think that is?

If we choose to eat meat, Judaism instructs us to take the animal's life in the most humane way possible. This is one reason for eating kosher meat. The animal is slaughtered in what is deemed to be the quickest way possible by the shochet (ritual slaughterer).

There is a traditional belief that God would actually prefer us to be vegetarians. When God created humanity, Adam and Eve were told they could eat fruit and plants. It is only after the flood that humans were permitted to eat meat. Keeping all this in mind, it is easy to see why Judaism frowns upon the sport of hunting.

What Is Kosher?

The word *kasher* means "fit" or "proper." It can apply to food, clothing, or even a situation. Usually it is refers to food. When a food is said to be kosher, this means that it is fit for a Jew to eat.

For example, the traditional rules of kashrut require the separation of meat and milk products as well as utensils used in their preparation. This comes from the biblical phrase "you shall not boil a lamb in its mother's milk." But this verse also shows the Torah's underlying concern for animal life even though it allows animals to be eaten. An animal must be slaughtered in a swift, painless manner specified by Jewish practice in order to be considered kosher. The remaining blood must be removed from the meat by salting. Over the centuries many intricate rules have developed regarding kashrut. They are not found in the Torah but were developed by rabbis interpreting the Torah.

Some people practice what is called biblical kashrut. This entails following only those laws of kashrut that appear in the

Shechitah ("slaughtering") of animals is carried out in accordance with humane Jewish laws. Only a properly qualified person, called a shochet, may perform shechitah. The meat is then inspected and certified as kosher. The kosher stamp shown here was used in a European Jewish community in the nineteenth century.

kosher

Two Israeli stamps.
Israel has created numerous bird sanctuaries to protect its winged friends.

שׁוֹחֵט
ritual slaughterer

**Vegetarian Resource Group
VRG**

Torah, such as the laws forbidding the consumption of pigs and shellfish. Whether traditional or biblical—or somewhere in-between—people who choose to keep kosher feel that fulfilling this mitzvah makes them more aware of the food they eat. For many, keeping kosher takes the necessary act of eating and gives it a greater spiritual meaning.

Though Jews feel that the method of killing animals used in kashrut is as humane as possible, in recent times some people have disagreed. Several countries have tried to outlaw kosher slaughtering in order to introduce an allegedly more humane method. This raises the issue of which method of slaughtering is humane: the one used in kashrut, which is performed with one swift, painless cut on a conscious animal, or the one used in nonkosher assembly-line slaughterhouses, which entails stunning the animal first.

Jews concerned about ethical issues raise another question about animals raised for food. Should an animal be considered kosher if it is treated inhumanely? Some animals are force-fed and spend their lives in feeding stalls. Oftentimes, chickens are cramped together and their beaks are cut off so they will not peck each other. Keeping animals in such conditions certainly seems to be tsa'ar ba'alei hayyim, and if so, shouldn't animals raised in this way be declared not kosher? What do you think?

Many Jews strive to fulfill the ideal of kindness to animals. They place great value on animal life, seeing it as being no different than human life. They believe that we can avoid being cruel to animals by abstaining from eating meat and wearing items made from animal products.

It is very challenging to be a Jew and not eat meat. Many Jewish holiday foods consist of meat dishes. One of the biggest challenges is conducting a Passover Seder. After all, one symbol is the egg and another is the shankbone. Today, there are vegetarian Haggadot that provide alternative symbols to be used on the Seder plate.

To Eat or Not to Eat
The Jewish vegetarian movement is growing steadily and is devoted to preventing tsa'ar ba'alei hayyim. There are many sources of information on vegetarianism from a Jewish per-

spective. One of the foremost is Micah Publications. The Vegetarian Resource Group recently put out a Jewish vegetarian cookbook.

There are many books and pamphlets by Jews interested in vegetarianism. Many of them survey Jewish food customs from around the world and introduce American Jews to food customs that are authentically Jewish but do not involve the taking of a life. For example, what do you do if your family traditionally breaks the Yom Kippur fast with a feast of meat and chicken? You might be interested in learning of the Iraqi Jewish tradition of breaking the fast with almond milk. You could find an also find alternative to chicken soup, and yes, there is vegetarian chopped liver. Much of this material can be obtained informally through the Internet.

If you are inclined to delve more deeply into what Judaism has to say about vegetarianism, the same organizations have collected and published the traditional source material on this subject, as well as essays by rabbis in all the major American movements.

The Jewish vegetarian movement is tied in to a spiritual movement called Jewish Renewal. This movement looks at alternatives in spirituality, and tries to make traditional and nontraditional spiritual modes available to all Jews. In exploring Jewish Renewal you could try meditation, or concentrate on Jewish mysticism, or explore Jewish issues from a feminist perspective. Taking on the mitzvot of bal tashhit and avoiding tsa'ar ba'alei hayyim would be another way of attaining heightened Jewish spirituality. After all, bringing us closer to God is the objective of all the mitzvot.

While the Torah tells us that we may make use of animals, we are also to take care of them. A lost animal is to be taken care of until its owner is found. That's a good Jewish reason for keeping a dog that has followed you home. The Ten Commandments teach us that even animals are to get Shabbat as a day of rest! As Judaism developed, more mitzvot concerning animals were added. The rabbis who wrote the Talmud decreed people may not eat until they have fed their animals.

Look back at the Noahide laws, discussed in the introduction. These are the laws, according to Jewish tradition, that all humanity is supposed to follow. One of them states that you shall not eat a limb from a living animal, a custom in many

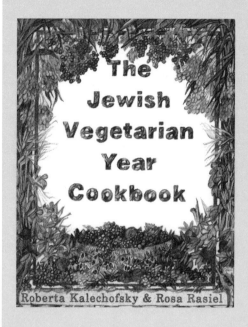

צִמְחוֹנִי

vegetarian

early societies. According to Jewish belief, tsa'ar ba'alei hayyim is incumbent upon everyone, not just Jews.

There are no Jewish organizations dealing solely with the treatment of animals. However, environmental groups like Shomrei Adamah and the Society for the Preservation of Nature are also concerned with animals.

Still, there are many ways in which we take the treatment of animals for granted. Animals are used to test different items that humans will use. Do you think it is proper to use animals for medical tests, as was done by the Hebrew University researcher seeking a medical cure? Is it permissible to let medical students practice surgery on puppies? Should biology classes be allowed to dissect earthworms and frogs? Is it all right to use animals to test cosmetics?

Sometimes mitzvot clash with each other. One of the most difficult aspects of avoiding tsa'ar ba'alei hayyim is deciding what to do when the mitzvah of pikuach nefesh, saving a human life, means that an animal will suffer. In which of the above cases is human life more important? In which cases is it more important to avoid tsa'ar ba'alei hayyim?

Animals and Pain

The issue of avoiding pain to animals has a long history in Jewish tradition. It is summarized in a nineteenth-century book called the *Kitzur Shulchan Aruch,* by Rabbi Solomon Ganzfried. Rabbi Ganzfried took the existing Jewish code of law, the sixteenth-century *Shulchan Aruch,* shortened it (that's what *kitzur* means), and simplified it. This easy-to-read code became immensely popular among Ashkenazi (European) Jews for its clear presentation of the mitzvot.

Drawing on centuries of Jewish tradition and law, here are a few things the *Kitzur Shulchan Aruch* (chap. 191) states about tsa'ar ba'alei hayyim:

191:1. According to the Torah it is forbidden to cause pain to any living creature. On the contrary, it is our obligation to relieve the pain of any creature.

191:3. It is forbidden to tie the legs of an animal or bird in a way that causes pain.

191:4. It is forbidden to place a bird on a nest of eggs of a different species. This is considered cruelty to animals.

The Biblical Zoo in Jerusalem

קִצּוּר שֻׁלְחָן עָרוּךְ
abbreviated Shulchan Aruch

How can these three examples be used to come up with a response to the use of animals in medical experiments? What about product testing on animals? Is it permitted, permitted within limits, or strictly forbidden?

As guardians of the earth we are also the caretakers of its animals. This means all animals: dogs, cats, guinea pigs, and hamsters as well as endangered species. Sometimes it is easier to save an animal that is far away, exotic, and of no immediate use to us.

Finally the words of the great twelfth-century Spanish rabbi and physician Moses Maimonides teach us much about the importance of kindness to animals. Maimonides, called Rambam in Hebrew, says that if we show kindness to animals, we are more likely to be kind and compassionate to other people. Do you agree that people who care for animals are also more concerned about one other?

Teachings from Tradition

If along a road you happen to find a bird's nest, in a tree or on the ground, with baby birds or eggs and the mother sitting over the babies or the eggs, do not take the mother together with her young.

<Devarim 22:6>

Even those things that might be considered unimportant, such as fleas, gnats and flies, are a part of the creation of the world. God carries out the Divine purpose through everything, even through a snake, even through a gnat, even through a frog.

<Beresheet Rabbah 10:7>

A person should not eat	אָסוּר לְאָדָם שֶׁיּאכַל
before	קֹדֶם
he feeds	שֶׁיִּתֵּן מַאֲכָל
his livestock	לִבְהֶמְתּוֹ

<Berachot 40a>

תַּלְמוּד תּוֹרָה

Talmud Torah:
Study

Why do I have to go to Hebrew school? It seems unfair that your friends get to play while you are sitting in class after a long day at school. When Sunday morning comes around, you'd probably prefer to sleep late or read the comics. Yet your parents take you to religious school.

Learning has always been an important part of being Jewish. That is one reason we are called *am ha-sefer,* "people of the book." Jewish books that are hundreds of years old tell us that children should begin to learn at the age of four or five. They also say that you should continue learning your whole life.

Discussions of what to study and at what age have also been going on among Jews for centuries. Rabbi Abaye, in the Talmud, reminisced about this in the pages of the Talmud: "Abaye said: My stepmother told me that a child of six is ready for Torah, at ten for Mishnah, at thirteen for a twenty-four-hour fast" (Ketubot 50a). How does this compare with what you learn and do in religious school?

Why is learning so important? The more you know about something, the better you are at it. The more you practice, the easier it gets. Think of the first time you tried to ride a bicycle. You probably didn't get very far. Now you are very proud because you can ride very easily. Hebrew school makes being

עַם הַסֵּפֶר

People of the Book

In the shtetl, boys and girls were taught separately. A female teacher instructs her pupils.

כִּתָּה אָלֶף
first grade

An outdoor classroom. Fresh air. Fresh ideas.

תַּלְמוּד תּוֹרָה
Torah study

Jewish easier. By learning and practicing, you become proud of all the Jewish things you know and can do. In *Kitah Alef* (alef class), you struggle through the alphabet; by the age of thirteen, you can read from the Torah and lead services!

Teaching the Teachers

Because learning is an important element in Jewish life, it is not surprising that Jewish texts cover all aspects of learning. The Talmud provides some teacher training by dividing students into four groups:

> Those who learn quickly and forget quickly; what they gain disappears in the loss. Those who learn slowly and forget slowly; their loss disappears in what is gained. Those who learn quickly and forget slowly; they receive a good portion. Those who learn slowly and forget quickly; they receive an evil portion.
> —Pirke Avot 4:15

Elsewhere in the Talmud, teachers are advised that no matter what the ability of the student, the teacher must repeat the lesson until the student understands it (Eruvin 54b).

The school itself must also be taken into consideration. First, you must make sure you live in a place that has a school. According to the Talmud (Shabbat 119a), a city without schools is doomed to destruction. Why do you think schools are considered so important?

Finally, there is a limit to the number of students that can be taught by one teacher at one time.

> The maximum number of students who should be placed with one teacher is twenty-five. If there are fifty, another teacher must be hired. If there are forty, a student assistant may be hired to help the teacher.
> —Bava Batra 21a

The Mitzvah of Talmud Torah

The Hebrew term *talmud torah* means "studying Torah." In this case, torah refers not only to the scroll we read at services but to the entire body of Jewish teachings. When you study in school you are preparing for a career. When you study in religious school you are preparing to be a responsible adult and to have a fulfilling life.

Sending you to school is a mitzvah your parents have to fulfill. Among the things Jewish tradition instructs your parents to do are these three: teach you Torah (so you can be a good, responsible person), learn a trade or profession (so that you can take care of yourself), and learn to swim (this could save your life).

One-Room Schoolhouse

Jewish education has been around for thousands of years—but not quite in the same way as today. Until the twentieth century, only boys got a formal education. At the age of three or four, boys in Eastern Europe were sent to a heder. This is a word meaning "room," and the heder was actually a one-room schoolhouse.

The boys would sit together on long benches, sharing books, and all reciting out loud. They would be in school all day, but they only studied Jewish topics: Hebrew, Bible, and prayers. As they got older they held discussions about what they read.

The schools were usually very crowded and poor. In the winter, the students would have wear their coats to keep warm. To make sure that youngsters would be excited about going to school, a very special first lesson was always planned. Drops of honey were put on the pages of the alefbet book. The boy would lick the honey as he learned the letters. This was to show him that learning was sweet.

New Schools in the New World

In early America, Jews hired private tutors to teach their children Jewish subjects. This meant that only the well-off Jewish families received a Jewish education. One woman thought this was unfair. Her name was Rebecca Gratz, and she came from a well-to-do family. In Philadelphia in 1838, she created the Jewish Sunday school.

Rebecca Gratz thought it was important for all Jewish children to learn about their heritage. The school she set up gave free classes to the Jewish children of Philadelphia. It met for four hours on Sunday. Soon Hebrew schools were opened in other cities. Some, like the Hebrew Free School in New York, did more than teach Jewish children. They also gave food and clothing to poor students. Because of Rebecca

חֶדֶר

one-room schoolhouse

An Israeli classroom.

Rebecca Gratz

• 99

יְשִׁיבָה

day school

Yeshiva University was founded in 1896. It began as the Yeshiva Rabbi Yitzhak Elchanan and has expanded into a complete university. It has a variety of professional schools including Albert Einstein Medical School. Yeshiva University ordains Orthodox rabbis, and trains educational directors for day and afternoon Hebrew schools.

Young Men's/Women's
Hebrew Association
YMHA/YWHA

חַברוּתָא

a fellowship

In 1873, Rabbi Isaac Mayer Wise founded the Hebrew Union College in Cincinnati, Ohio. It was the first American institution of higher Jewish education and for the training of Reform rabbis. Today the HUC has branches in New York, Los Angles and Israel. The Hebrew Union College is a powerful voice for Reform Jewry.

Gratz, many children who had no opportunity to go to school were given a chance to fulfill the mitzvah of learning.

In modern America we have many different types of Jewish schools. There is the afternoon school, which meets after school and on the weekends. There is the Jewish day school. It takes the place of regular school. You learn all the regular subjects, such as reading, math, and science. You also spend time every day learning Hebrew, Bible, and other Jewish subjects.

The major Jewish religious movements in America each have their own day schools. An Orthodox day school is usually called a yeshiva. The Conservative movement runs the Solomon Schechter schools, and the Reform movement also runs a number of day schools. There are, as well, many independent day schools.

Jewish education is also provided in other ways. Many kids look forward to spending the summer in Jewish camps. There are day camps and sleepaway camps. The camps are usually run by a Jewish community center, a YMHA/YWHA, a religious movement, or some other Jewish organization. All of them have the usual camp programs: swimming, hikes, arts and crafts. They also have special Jewish activities, such as games in Hebrew, Israeli dancing, religious services, and even special counselors from Israel. There are even Jewish camps for special-needs students.

In Judaism, adult learning is also very important. That is why synagogues have adult education programs. Synagogues are not the only institutions with adult education programs. Jewish community centers also offer many courses. Some of the classes are for grownups who never had a chance to go to Hebrew school when they were young. Other classes are for people who have studied for many years. In some classes you watch movies, or cook, or listen to music. All Jewish classes have a very important goal: learning about and enjoying your Jewish heritage.

An important aspect of *talmud torah* is that all Jews can study together. The elderly can study with the very young, the advanced student can study with the beginner. The traditional method of study is in a small group of two or three people called a *hevruta* (fellowship). Those who study together in small groups are able to cooperate and help one another. One person may be better at reading or at Hebrew, another may be more creative, a third could be a good problem solver. In Jewish study, everyone has something to offer.

Some religious schools try to give their students a chance to teach what they have learned. Many Hebrew schools welcome back students who have become Bar or Bat Mitzvah to help out as teaching assistants in class or as private tutors. If you choose to fulfill the mitzvah of *talmud torah* by becoming a teacher as well a student, you will discover the reason for this saying: "I have learned much from my teachers and my colleagues, but I have learned most from my students" (Ta'anit 7a).

A New Curriculum

Rabbi Israel Salanter (1810–1883) was a man greatly concerned with the moral breakdown caused by poverty and social problems in the Jewish communities of Eastern Europe. His response was to try and strengthen the individual's moral base. As he once said: "Usually we worry about our own well-being and our neighbor's soul; we should rather worry about our neighbor's material well-being and our own souls."

Rabbi Salanter tried to fulfill these words by setting out a course of moral study, called *musar* in Hebrew. The idea was to read Jewish ethical literature that stressed dealing with people in an ethical manner. Unfortunately, the experiment failed. The established leaders of the community were not about to take advice.

Still convinced that the Jewish community was in a moral decline and, as well, threatened by new secular teachings, Rabbi Salanter tried a different tack. If adults were "too old to learn," it made sense to teach children.

Through the efforts of followers of Rabbi Salanter, a new type of yeshiva was established, where the primary purpose was to model and teach ethical behavior. This was done through a series of spiritual exercises. The teacher would choose some biblical verses or sayings that taught a moral lesson. The teacher and students would chant these sayings to a melody, the idea being that the melody would bring about an emotional as well as an intellectual response. This type of study was also meant to create a sense of unity among the students.

The Jewish Theological Seminary

Solomon Schechter
In 1861 Rabbi Sabato Morais and his associates founded the Jewish Theological Seminary. It was first headed by the scholar Solomon Schechter. He gathered an impressive faculty and gave form to the Conservative movement. The Jewish Theological Seminary ordains Conservative rabbis and graduates Jewish scholars.

מוּסָר

ethics

Sometimes musar learning would take place in a dimly lit room, which added to its meditative quality. In some schools, students would set up their own study groups, chanting together and providing one other with emotional support. In some instances, the teacher would choose an ethical theme each week.

One offshoot of musar-style education involved an unusual type of self-discipline that confronted the student with his own emotions. Exercises included being dressed poorly in a room with well-dressed people, or going into a store and asking for an item that one could buy at a different store. The idea was to teach students to be less selfish and vain, and not to care about material things.

Many modern yeshivot use musar-style learning. Do you think it is possible to teach people to behave ethically? Is it easier or more difficult to do this in a religious school?

Two heads, one book.

Teachings from Tradition

Take to heart these instructions with which I charge you this day. Impress them upon your children. Recite them when you are at home and when you are away, when you lie down and when you rise up. Bind them as a sign upon your hand and let them be a symbol on our forehead. Inscribe them on the doorposts of your house and on your gates

<Devarim 6:6–9>

Do not say: "When I have free time I will study." Perhaps you will have no free time.

<Pirke Avot 2:5>

Study leads to action.

<Kiddushin 40a>

A town that has no schoolchildren is doomed to destruction.

<Shabbat 119b>

A person should not say I will read in order to be called a scholar; rather do it out of love and honor will follow.

<Nedarim 62a>

Students increase a teacher's wisdom and broaden the teacher's mind. The sages said: "I have learned much from my teachers, even more from my colleagues, but I have learned the most from my students."

<Rambam, Hilchot Talmud Torah, 5:13>

Scholars	תַּלְמִידֵי חֲכָמִים
increase	מַרְבִּים
peace	שָׁלוֹם
in the world	בָּעוֹלָם

<Talmud>

שָׁלוֹם בַּיִת

Shlom Bayit: Family Harmony

There is a story about a Roman woman who was told that God had created the world in six days. "What has God been doing since then?" she asked. A rabbi replied: "Ever since, God has been busy making marriages." This story implies that making a good marriage is much more difficult than creating a world. It also shows that there is an unseen partner in marriage and family life, God.

The Mitzvah of Shlom Bayit

In Judaism, family life is called *shlom bayit*. This literally means "the peace of the home," and refers to the relationship between husband and wife. If there is peace and harmony at home, then it is easier to face other difficulties. Shelom bayit does not come by itself. It is something that both partners in a marriage must work at all the time. That is why shlom bayit is so important a mitzvah.

People who live together, such as family members, see each other at good times and at bad. It is during difficult times that shlom bayit can be most helpful. One of the most important aspects of shlom bayit is mutual respect. When we get angry, we tend to raise our voices, to yell, to stop listening. Shlom bayit requires us to try and control our anger, to listen

Israeli stamp in honor of the Jewish family heritage

שָׁלוֹם בַּיִת

family harmony

to each other and let others speak. This way, there is respect even at times when there is anger.

Marriage Counseling

Throughout the centuries, marriage has been looked upon as the ideal state for Jewish men and women. Yet it was always recognized that difficulties arise in every marriage. The writers of Jewish texts were keen observers of human life. They placed their observations within the context of Jewish tradition as reflected in their time and place. Here is some marital advice from Moses Maimonides, the Rambam. Does any of it still hold today? Are any of his comments only a reflection of life in the twelfth century?

According to Rambam, in *Mishneh Torah,* Hilchot Nashim 15:19—20, a husband and wife have certain obligations toward each other. A man is required to honor his wife more than himself and love her as himself. If he has money, he is to be generous to his wife according to his wealth. He must not frighten her. In talking with his wife, he should be gentle. He should not be prone to sadness or anger.

The wife is required to honor her husband greatly and hold him in awe. She is to arrange all her affairs according to his instructions. She is to view her husband as royalty and behave as he wishes her to. She is to avoid anything that is hateful to her husband.

Maimonides realized that many marital tensions have underlying reasons, often tied to work. Here too, he provides advice. Again, is this advice is dated, or does it still make sense today?

A husband may not force his wife to move from a good location to a bad one, unless he wants to make aliyah (move to Israel). If he wants to move there and she doesn't, he must grant her a divorce. If they are living in Israel and the husband wants to leave, but the wife does not, she cannot be compelled to leave Israel (*Mishneh Torah*, Hilchot Nashim 13:18–20).

Business travel can put a strain on family life. A wife has the right to restrict her husband's business traveling if it will affect their marriage. She also has the right to prevent him from changing occupations if doing so would keep him away from home (*Mishneh Torah*, Hilchot Nashim 14:2). (A mod-

נִשּׂוּאִין

marriage

A ketubah (marriage contract), 1838. This document is written in Aramaic. and must bear the signatures of two witnesses.

English wedding tray, 1769. The inscription reads: "Let God rejoice over you, as a bridegroom rejoices with his bride."

A Bokharan wedding ceremony in Israel. Under the tallit canopy, East meets West in the dress of the bride and groom.

ern example would be if he wanted to become an airline pilot.)

Even if people try their best, they may not be able to settle their differences. There are places to turn to in the Jewish community to receive help in achieving shlom bayit.

People who are having a problem at home are urged to seek outside help. Sometimes, a third person can have a clearer view of a solution to the problem. Rabbis are always available for counseling. Some rabbis are professional counselors. If the rabbi does not have a counseling degree, then the person seeking help will be referred to another counselor, usually at Jewish Family Services (JFS).

There are JFS offices in most Jewish communities. They help couples who are having marital difficulties. The JFS personnel are trained counselors who work with both spouses either separately or together. Counselors can also be of help for other family members, such as parents and children who do not get along with each other. JFS also helps people who have trouble with alcohol or drugs. In some cities, JFS finds Jewish foster and adoptive families for Jewish children. If a personal problem is preventing a family from achieving shlom bayit, Jewish Family Services is the primary resource that can help.

In what way is this type of counseling different from what is offered by a school counselor? A Jewish counselor has the same training as any other counselor. The difference is that a counselor at a Jewish organization brings Judaism into the process. Judaism and Jewish mitzvot, especially those between human beings, are at the center of Jewish counseling. The goal of Jewish counseling is to help each family achieve shlom bayit.

Twelve Steps

Problems in families have many causes and symptoms. People bring their own personalities and histories into a relationship. At times, people handle problems in ways that are harmful to them and their families. Some turn to substance abuse and develop an addiction. Others may turn to violence.

In each of these cases there are programs to help people stop the abuse. There are also programs to help them cope with abusers. Within the Jewish community, such programs may be found at Jewish Family Services. There are also secular organizations that have helped many Jews, such as Alcoholics Anonymous (AA).

To take part in a self-help program, an individual must first acknowledge that a problem exists. Then the person must be willing to deal with the problem. Self-help groups provide support from people who have personally had a problem with alcoholism or drug abuse and dealt with it. These programs are called twelve-step programs because they present a model of twelve steps to handling your problem.

An important part of such programs is an acknowledgment of a Greater Being that one can turn to. Religion is used as a source of support. For this reason, some chapters have a specifically Jewish approach. They may be housed in a temple or a Jewish community center. They provide Jewish prayers as part of the meetings instead of the standard Christian Lord's Prayer that is usually a part of such gatherings.

There are also twelve-step programs run by Jewish organizations. One such nationwide group is Jewish Alcoholics, Chemically Dependent Persons and Significant Others (JACS). In order to achieve shlom bayit, JACS provides help not only for the abuser but for other family members.

When All Else Fails

Sometimes, after trying and trying, a married couple finds that they simply do not get along anymore. In Judaism, divorce is permitted. Just as marriage is a religious ceremony before God, so too is a Jewish divorce (*get*). Divorce is viewed as a way to correct a mistake. If a couple has truly tried, and failed to achieve shlom bayit, they are better off starting again. In Judaism, if both partners agree to a divorce, they are then free to strive for shlom bayit in another marriage.

The Good and the Bad

As mentioned previously, marriage is the ideal state in Jewish tradition. A great many customs and laws have arisen to promote and protect marriages. Sometimes they work and other times they backfire. Today, those who follow traditional Jewish law must still struggle with the issues that have developed over time.

**Alcoholics Anonymous
AA**

**Jewish Alcoholics, Chemically Dependent Persons and Significant Others
JACS**

גֵּט

writ of divorce

כְּתוּבָּה

ketubah

The Jewish marriage contract (ketubah) developed centuries ago as a protection for the wife. Within Judaism, it is a legally binding contract that provides for the woman's economic needs.

Divorce arose as a response to necessity. While it works within halachah (Jewish law), it is not ideal. In traditional Judaism, only a husband can initiate a divorce, though the wife has to be the one to accept it. At times, where the couple does not get along, the husband refuses to grant a Jewish divorce out of spite. In observant communities the only recourse is to shun the recalcitrant husband. The community will boycott his business. Often these tactics do not work. In Israel, such husbands can be jailed until they agree to give the wife a get, a Jewish divorce.

The Conservative movement has worked out a solution within their halachah. In the Conservative ketubah (marriage contract), there is a clause stating that in case of divorce, either husband or wife can approach a Conservative Bet Din (religious court) and request a divorce. Since this is stated in the ketubah, both husband and wife have agreed to it, and either may initiate the process.

Like other ancient cultures, Judaism once had the custom of childhood betrothals. Your parents would decide whom you would marry while you were still very young. Obviously, this does not hold true for us today. Yet there are still some Jewish communities where childhood betrothal exists.

There is one issue which has yet to be resolved in a religious manner. This is the case of the agunah. An agunah is a woman whose husband has disappeared. Perhaps he was lost at sea, perhaps he just walked out on her. Unless proof can be given that the husband is no longer alive, she is considered still married. This issue was a major problem at the close of World War II. Many Holocaust survivors were not permitted to remarry within Judaism because they could not show proof that their husbands had died in concentration camps. Within the various religious movements, and as part of women's groups, there are efforts being made to come up with a solution to the problem of the agunah.

Differences and Similarities
In modern America, not every Jew marries another Jew. Some

Jews marry persons of a different religion. This is called inter-marriage. From a traditional religious perspective, it is not considered the ideal situation. Nevertheless, the Jewish community has responded to this issue.

Recognizing that marriage is difficult enough, the added factor of two faiths places additional stress on a family. The Reform movement's program for helping interfaith families is called Outreach. It runs many activities to welcoming inter-married couples into the Jewish community, from introductory programs that teach about Judaism to discussions on how to raise Jewish children in a home where the parents are of two faiths. The Conservative movement has a program called *Kiruv*, Hebrew for "bringing closer." Here too a place is made for the family in the Jewish community. Both movements stress the importance of raising the children in one religion, and providing formal education in that religion.

Happily Ever After

The concept of *shlom bayit* is the ideal to strive for in families. We know that it is difficult and cannot be accomplished alone. That is why there is always help available, through self-help and support groups, through professional agencies like Jewish Family Services, and through the religious leaders at your synagogue.

Honor Your Father and Your Mother

There can be no *shlom bayit* if there is no *kebud av v'em*, "honor for your father and mother." Jewish tradition teaches that you must honor your father and your mother in the same manner as you revere God.

כְּבוּד אָב וְאֵם

honoring your father
and mother

A happy Jewish home means *shlom bayit*: it means a center of love and cooperation; it means a home in which you drink in ideas and ethics, which will mold your thinking, your attitudes and your actions; it means a place where the Fifth Commandment, "honor your father and your mother" is always obeyed. The Talmud also says that it means a home where parents love their children and treat them with gentleness and respect.

Teachings from Tradition

Therefore a man leaves his father and mother and clings to his wife, and they become one flesh.　　<Genesis 2:24>

If a man divorces his first wife even the altar sheds tears.
<Gittin 90b>

Many get married, most succeed, some fail.
<Bamidbar Rabbah >

It was the custom in Judah that a cedar tree was planted when a boy was born and an acacia tree when a girl was born. When they grew up and married their wedding canopy was made of the branches from both trees.
<From the seven blessings recited at a wedding, based on Jeremiah 33:10–11>

There will again be heard	עוֹד יִשָּׁמַע
in the cities of Judah	בְּעָרֵי יְהוּדָה
and the streets of Jerusalem	וּבְחוּצוֹת יְרוּשָׁלַיִם
the voice of joy	קוֹל שָׂשׂוֹן
and the voice gladness,	וְקוֹל שִׂמְחָה,
the voice of the groom	קוֹל חָתָן
and the voice of the bride.	וְקוֹל כַּלָּה

<Gittin 57a>

לְשׁוֹן הָרַע

Leshon ha-Ra:
The Evil Tongue

"MARTIAN HELPS STUDENT WITH SCIENCE PROJECT," "VOICE OF ELVIS COACHES TEAM TO VICTORY." If you've ever had a long wait at a supermarket checkout, you've probably seen headlines similar to this. The magazine racks at the checkout are filled with such attention-grabbing headlines. Lots of people buy these papers too. These newspapers and magazines contain stories ranging from the unbelievable to "true confessions" to gossip. Such things have always been popular. Even serious newspapers carry gossip columns. Television talk-shows increase yearly, and most deal with people exposing their deepest secrets in front of millions. In fact, whenever stations want to boost their ratings, they make sure to run gossipy "special reports" on the local news. Viewers seem to be more interested in gossip than are in issues of war and peace, our social condition, or economic problems.

Celebrity status is important for actors, athletes and politicians. Actors need fans, sport figures need to spur attendance, and politicians are hungry for votes. Anyone who depends on public recognition to earn a living or get elected, has to expect close scrutiny. However, at some point the individual no matter how famous is entitled to have a private life of his or her own.

They and their families are hurt when false rumors and malicious gossip lashon ha-ra begins to circulate about their private lives. Lashon ha-ra can also hurt products and businesses.

Gossip columns, televisions exposes, and unsubstantiated and untraceable rumors on the Internet have the potential of creating human, business and political tragedies.

A book about the evil of gossip.

The Two Tongues
The Talmud tells about Rabbi Gamliel, who sent a servant to purchase and bring back the best and the worst foods in the market.

Front page of the English edition of the
Forward, July 5, 1996.

יִשְׂרָאֵל שֶׁלָנוּ.

newspaper

Jewish Telegraphic Agency
JTA

When the servant returned Rabbi Gamliel said "Please show me the worst food you bought." The servant opened his basket and showed the tongue of an ox.

"Now" said the rabbi, "show me the best food that you bought."

Once again the servant opened his basket and showed Rabbi Gamliel another ox tongue. At this point Rabbi Gamliel angrily snapped, "I sent you to buy the best and the worst food in the market, and you brought me two same tongues. Explain yourself!"

Gamliel's servant cleverly replied, "Rabbi, there is nothing worse than a tongue when it speaks only leshon ha-ra, and nothing is better than a tongue that only speaks words of wisdom and kindness."

All the Jewish News That's Fit to Print

In addition to mass circulation newspapers, there are many special-interest ones. The Jewish community in the United States has been publishing newspapers for a long time. Even within the American Jewish community, there are special interest newspapers. Israelis living in America may read a newspaper called *Yisrael Shelanu* ("Our Israel"). It is published in New York but distributed to Israelis around the country. The focus of *Yisrael Shelanu* is news from Israel and activities of interest to Israelis living in America.

At the beginning of the twentieth century, many Yiddish-speaking immigrants landed on the Lower East Side of New York. The newspaper that helped them adjust to life in the New World was the *Jewish Daily Forward*, published in Yiddish. They read it for news, ads, poetry, stories by writers such as future Nobel Prize winner Isaac Bashevis Singer, and a popular advice column called the "Bintel Brief." The *Forward* still exists today. In keeping up with changes in the Jewish world, the *Forward* also publishes a weekly paper in English. It provides in-depth coverage of matters of Jewish interest.

The Jewish communities of North America have many papers that provide local coverage. While many also have national reporters, all these papers subscribe to a news service called the Jewish Telegraphic Agency (JTA). This is the Jewish equivalent of the Associated Press, providing news coverage of Jewish interest from around the world.

The JTA was started in 1914 in the Hague, moving to London in 1919. The headquarters moved once again, in 1922, to New York. While newspapers subscribe to it for the wire services, the JTA needs outside funding in order to survive. Much of its money comes from Jewish welfare funds.

Aside from newspapers, the Jewish community supports many magazines. Organizations like Hadassah and the different religious movements have their own publications. There are also magazines with specific political leanings, such as *Commentary* (conservative) and *Tikkun* (liberal). The articles in these publications appeal to the general community as well as the Jewish one. *Lilith* is a Jewish feminist magazine. There are many others you can find in your public or synagogue library. They include *Moment, Midstream,* and the *Jerusalem Report.*

With the rise of the worldwide web, Jewish publications have gone on-line. You can subscribe to the *Jerusalem Post* and receive a daily update of the news from Israel. Many specialty publications are also available on the internet. Why do you think there is such a diversity of publications in the Jewish community?

The Mitzvah of Avoiding Leshon ha-Ra

Gossip is fun, so what's the big deal? The problem is, that gossip always has a victim: the person being discussed. It doesn't matter whether the gossip is true or not; the way in which it is discussed is harmful. In Judaism, gossip is called *leshon ha-ra,* which means "the evil tongue."

In Judaism, we are well aware of the joy of gossip. The Talmud states that the one commandment every single person has broken is the commandment not to gossip. Avoiding gossip is so important that it appears in the Siddur. At the conclusion of the Amidah we pray to God to "guard my tongue from evil" and protect us from evil speech against us.

There are actually several different types of evil speech which it is a mitzvah to avoid.

Leshon ha-ra, "the evil tongue," specifically refers to spreading rumors or gossip that are true! Why is it wrong to spread true information? Something can be true and still cause harm. Think of something embarrassing that has happened to

The cover page of *Commentary Magazine,* dated **February 1997.** *Commentary* is one of the leading journals of political thought, published by the American Jewish Committee.

לָשׁוֹן הָרַע

evil tongue

מוֹצִיא שֵׁם רַע

giving someone a bad name

רְכִילוּת

gossip

you. How would you feel if everybody knew about it?

Motzi shem ra, "giving someone a bad name," refers to spreading gossip that is untrue. You can do this if you repeat a story you heard. How do you know if the story is true or not? Sometimes we get such pleasure out of telling a story that we don't care whether or not it is true. Other times, we deliberately set out to make someone look bad. Perhaps we are jealous of the friends that person has. Maybe we want that person's job, or it could be part of a political campaign. Even if it's "just business" or "just politics," it is anything but "just" Jewish.

The third type of gossip is called rehilut. This is the normal type of gossip most people are guilty of. It is part of everyday conversation and small talk: "Did you hear about so-and-so . . . ?" Rehilut also involves invading a person's privacy in order to find out personal and sometimes negative things about them.

The mitzvah of avoiding leshon ha-ra goes beyond avoiding such talk. Part of the commandment is not to listen to gossip either. The listener is an active participant and encourages the speaker. Listening to gossip can be as enjoyable as telling the story.

Sometimes issues are not so clear-cut. Can a joke be considered leshon ha-ra? A joke may not have a specific person as a victim. Yet jokes can denigrate entire groups of people. While humor is greatly appreciated in Judaism, jokes that hurt others fall into the category of leshon ha-ra.

Jewish News or Gossip?

Within the Jewish community the issue of leshon ha-ra arises in many ways. Every major Jewish community has a Jewish newspaper. The paper focuses on news and issues of Jewish interest. It contains international, national, and local stories. It carries letters and editorials. It operates under the same laws and philosophy as other American newspapers, including the idea of the public's right to know.

What happens if there is a scandal in a Jewish agency or a synagogue? What is the responsibility of the Jewish newspaper? Should the paper follow the philosophy of the public's right to know, or should it "answer to a higher authority"? If you were the editor of a Jewish newspaper and you had a story that one of the community's leaders had lied on a resume, how would you handle it?

Help Wanted

Printing was invented in Germany toward the end of the fifteenth century. Jewish printing began soon afterward in Italy. The chief printer of Jewish books was the Soncino family. The present-day Soncino Press, a major publisher of Jewish books, was named in its honor.

The colophon of the Soncino Press.

Surprisingly, Jewish women were very active in printing in the early centuries. Usually they were the daughters in a family business or widows taking over a late husband's work. Among the women printers were Donna Reyna in sixteenth-century Constantinople; Raizel, the wife of Fishel from Cracow; and two sisters, Rebecca and Rachel, the daughters of Isaac ben Judah Judels in seventeenth-century Germany.

We have names and information about many early printers because it was traditional for the printer to include such details on a page called a colophon. Among other things, the printer would ask to be forgiven for any printing errors. Printing was considered a holy task. The one thing you would not find in the colophons of the early press are examples of leshon ha-ra against rival printers.

Synagogues face similar problems with regard to gossip. Synagogue members must pay dues. Should a synagogue publish a list thanking paid-up members in its bulletin? By implication, this would tell everyone in the synagogue who had not paid their dues. As president of a synagogue, what would you do? In order to function, you need the dues from every member, but is it gossiping to let everyone know who has paid and who has not?

Suppose a synagogue has dismissed an office employee. A new employer calls for a reference. At what point does an honest answer turn into bad-mouthing the former employee? How would you handle such a call if you were the rabbi?

Where Has All the Gossip Gone?

Keep track of all the gossip items you come across in one week. How much of the evening news is gossip—and how much is truly news? Which is more memorable? How much of your conversation with friends consists of gossip? When you are not gossiping, what are you discussing with friends?

See if avoiding leshon ha-ra can help you attain a greater appreciation for others. Perhaps you will look at someone differently if you are not prejudiced by someone else's impression of that person. Maybe you will discover that you have things to offer your friends besides juicy gossip. In following this mitzvah you not only avoid belittling others, you do not belittle God. You are fulfilling the Jewish belief that all people are to be treated with respect since everyone is created *be-tzelem elohim*, "in God's image."

Guard My Tongue from Evil

Aside from the daily prayer that asks for God's help in avoiding slander, Jewish texts have strong opinions about those who engage in leshon ha-ra. In the Talmud (Arachin 15b), slander is called the third tongue because "it slays three people: the speaker, the spoken to, and the spoken of."

We are also warned against other transgressions of speech.

"Do not promise something to a child and not fulfill the promise, for this teaches the child to lie" (Sukkot 46b). Lying is a very serious offense: "There are seven classes of thieves, chief among them is the one who steals the mind of others [by lying]" (Tosefta Bava Kamma 7:8).

It is even "forbidden to create a false impression, that is, to deceive anyone, Jew or non-Jew, even by words alone" (*Kitzur Shulchan Aruch* 63:4). Interestingly, we may create a false impression without being aware of it. For example, if you go into a store, try on an outfit, and ask the price, but never intended to buy it, this is a giving a false impression (Bava Metzia 56–57).

Finally, the literature of musar tackles the ethical issue of dealing with other human beings, the foundation of which is dealing with others honestly, respectfully, and with dignity. *Sha'arei Teshuvah*, a work by Rabbi Jonah ben Abraham Gerondi (1200–1263), is one of the earliest books to deal with such questions. Rabbi Gerondi saw slander as one of the ten greatest sins of his time. *Sha'arei Teshuvah* deals with repentance and forgiveness, and ultimately advises people on ways to avoid injuring the dignity of other persons.

שַׁעֲרֵי תְּשׁוּבָה
Gates of Repentance

Teachings from Tradition

Do not be a talebearer among your people

<Vayikra 19:16>

Who is the one who is eager for life, who desires years of good fortune? Guard your tongue from evil and your lips from deceitful speech. Seek integrity and pursue it.

<Psalms 34:13–15>

A healing tongue is a tree of life but a devious one makes for a broken spirit.

<Proverbs 15:4>

For lack of wood a fire goes out, and without a fault-finding person quarrelling stops. Charcoal for embers and wood for fire, and a quarrelsome person for kindling strife. The words of a fault-finder are bruising, they penetrate one's innermost parts.

<Proverbs 26: 20–22>

My God, guard my tongue from evil and my lips from speaking deceitfully. Let my soul be silent before those who curse me, and let me be (humble) as dust before all.

<Siddur, based on Berachot 17a>

The gossiper	הָאוֹמֵר לְשׁוֹן הָרָע
destroys three people:	הוּא הוֹרֵג שְׁלוֹשָׁה:
himself,	הַמְּסַפְּרוֹ
the listener,	וְהַמְקַבְּלוֹ
and the victim	וּמִי שֶׁנֶּאֱמַר עָלָיו.

<Midrash Tehillim>

הִדּוּר מִצְוָה

Hiddur Mitzvah:
Beautifying the Mitzvah

The Chagall windows in the Hadassah–Hebrew University Medical Center took two years to complete. The final work was 12 windows, representing the 12 tribes of Israel. Each panel is a visual discription of a tribe based on the blessings given by Jacob and Moses.

The windows are positioned on all four sides of the synagogue, exactly the way the tribes traveled during the 40 years in the desert.

The above window represents the tribe of Levi.

People everywhere have always had the desire to beautify their surroundings. People decorate their homes, their clothing, even themselves. We have ancient examples of decorated pottery. There are samples of finely woven cloth from many different times and places. Art is a common form of expression in all societies.

Art has often been devoted to religious themes. The cathedrals and stained glass windows of medieval Europe are examples of this. Possibly the most famous example would be the ceiling of the Sistine Chapel in Rome. The artist Michelangelo had to lie flat on his back beneath the ceiling for four years, 1508–1512, painting nine scenes from the book of Genesis. He started with the first day of creation and ended with the story of the flood. He also painted images of different prophets. Michelangelo had been given this assignment by the pope. Why paint a church ceiling? To provide the worshippers with a sense of awe and holiness.

Within Judaism, there is an appreciation for the power art has as an aid to spirituality. In Exodus 15:2 we read: "This is my God, and I will praise God." Over the centuries Jewish sages have provided interpretations of what is meant by praising God. As they point out, God may be praised through prayer, through music, or through art. The rabbis suggested that *hiddur mitzvah* means making yourself beautiful by performing mitzvot. As an example they cite the mitzvah of decorating the sukkah.

Appreciating Beauty

Judaism provides a number of outlets for us to appreciate the beautiful and the unusual. One of the simplest ways of doing this is by reciting a blessing. There are special blessings you can say on seeing a rainbow or lightning, on encountering unusual animals, and even when you see an important person or a very wise person!

The Torah also teaches about works of art. The Tabernacle that the children of Israel built in the wilderness was to be made of different materials, colors, and textures. A man named Bezalel received divine inspiration to produce works of art to decorate the Tabernacle. The Bezalel School in modern Israel is named after this biblical figure.

A picture of the ancient Tabernacle.

> See, Adonai has singled out by name Bezalel, son of Uri son of Hur of the tribe of Judah. God has endowed him with a divine spirit of skill, ability, and knowledge in every kind of craft and has inspired him to make designs for work in gold, silver and copper, to cut stones for setting and to carve wood—to work in every kind of designer's craft—and to give directions.
>
> Exodus 35:30–33

Bezalel and other talented artists were responsible for the construction of the Tabernacle.

> Then all the skilled among those engaged in the work made the Tabernacle of ten tapestries, which they made of fine twisted linen, blue, purple, and crimson yarns; into these they worked the designs of cherubim. . . . They made the screen for the entrance of the Tabernacle, of blue, purple, and crimson yarns, and fine twisted linen, done in embroidery.
>
> Exodus 36:8, 37:37

They even made specially decorated garments for Aaron and his sons, the priests.

מִשְׁכָּן

tabernacle

On the hem of the robe they made pomegranates of blue, purple, and crimson yarns, twisted. They also made bells of pure gold and attached the bells between the pomegranates all around the hem of the robe.

Exodus 39:24

הִדּוּר מִצְוָה

beautifying a mitzvah

Today many skilled artists also strive to make beautiful ritual objects. When you become a Bar or Bat Mitzvah you may receive your own tallit or kippah. You will see that there is a wide variety of such items, each reflecting the taste and approach of a different artist and designs.

The Idea of Hiddur Mitzvah

In Judaism, using art for religious purposes is called hiddur mitzvah, "beautifying the mitzvah." If you look around your home or synagogue you will find many examples of hiddur mitzvah. Here are some items to examine: the Torah cover, a tallit, a mezuzah, a kiddush cup, a ketubah, a baby-naming certificate, a havdalah candle. Can you find other items?

Why bother decorating things? Try this experiment. Go into a bookstore and find a book that is available in several different editions from different publishers. Look at the decorative jackets of several versions of the same work (Mark Twain's *Tom Sawyer* or Louisa May Alcott's *Little Women*, for instance). If you were planning to buy a copy of this book, which one would you choose? Chances are, a good part of your decision would be based on how attractive the jacket is. Advertisers are well aware that consumers tend to purchase products presented in an appealing manner. That is why they use artistic ads and packaging to draw you to buy their product, whether a book or a box of cereal.

What's So Important About Fancy-Shmancy?

The way an object looks draws your attention. It stirs a reaction in you. This is true of everyday items you find in the store, and is equally true of religious items. Using an attractively decorated religious object will also stir a reaction in you. Hopefully, the reaction will enhance your enjoyment of the mitzvah you are performing.

Hiddur mitzvah takes the performance of a mitzvah to a higher level. It is the difference between getting a present that

Oriental Torah case, made of silver in 1860. The holy scroll was made of deerskin in the 17th century.

is not gift-wrapped and one that is. While both are exciting, the latter is more so.

Instead of drinking wine from just any cup for Kiddush, you could use a decorated cup, perhaps one that has the blessing written on it or is decorated with Shabbat symbols. Instead of lighting the Hanukah candles in a simple menorah, you could use one that is shaped like Jerusalem or is made up of Maccabees holding each candle. Perhaps you will spend more time just looking at the object, thinking of the special meaning of the occasion.

There are hundreds of artists who spend their time creating items to enhance our enjoyment of mitzvot. Among them are potters, glassblowers, calligraphers, weavers, painters, woodworkers, and candlemakers. Today, there are even artists who have revived the old Eastern European Jewish art of paper-cutting. You can buy their works at your synagogue's gift shop, at a local Jewish store, or through catalogues.

There are different styles of Jewish art. How can you tell whether a Seder plate was made in Israel or in the United States? Can you tell the difference between a mezuzah made in California or New York?

Enjoy all the religious articles you come into contact with, the way they look and feel.

If you really want to take the concept of hiddur mitzvah to a higher level, create some decorative religious articles yourself!

Cut On the Dotted Line

A popular Jewish art form which almost disappeared in this century is paper-cutting. Designs were cut into a piece of paper with a knife to make a picture. Often the picture was very elaborate and intricate.

Jewish paper-cuts had some standard themes. Menorah paper-cuts were popular in North Africa and the Middle East. Sometimes the paper-cuts had many layers. The branches of the menorot had inscriptions written on them.

Paper-cuts were very popular in Eastern Europe. There were special paper-cuts called *sheveetee* that were used to decorate windows on the holiday of Shavuot. The paper-cut known as a mizrach was made up of the Hebrew word mizrach (meaning "east") surrounded by decorations. It was

An example of a paper-cut design.

שְׁוִיתִי
paper cutting

מִזְרָח
East

Judah L. Magnes Museum

Jewish museums collect and exhibit works of art historical artifacts. The Jewish Museum in New York and the Judah L. Magnes Museum in Berkeley, California, are two important exhibit centers

סוֹפֵר

scribe

ס פְרֵי תּוֹרָה
ת פְּלִין
מ זוּזוֹת

סְתַּם

These tools are used in writing a Torah scroll. Here you see the inkwell, the reeds their case, quills, and sinews (of kosher animals) for sewing parchment sheets together.

When a scribe (sofer) writes a Torah scroll, he rules guidelines with the blunt edge, and divides each parchment sheet into sections. Every Torah scroll must be entirely handwritten.

placed on the eastern wall of the house so that the residents would know where to face when they prayed. Even Simchat Torah flags were made from paper-cuts!

While it flourished for hundreds of years, this art was almost forgotten in the early years of the twentieth century. Recently, however, as they began to explore lesser-known parts of their heritage, several artists have revived the art of paper-cutting. It is now possible to buy paper-cut works in many stores and galleries specializing in Jewish art.

From A to Z

Hebrew calligraphy serves both an artistic and a halachic purpose. Calligraphy is the art of writing in a highly ornamental, decorative manner. When a Jewish couple gets married, their ketubah may be individually calligraphed and decorated by an artist. They may receive presents of calligraphed blessings. A Bar or Bat Mitzvah Torah portion may be calligraphed and framed as a present.

Calligraphy plays an important role in Judaism. The writing of Torah scrolls, tefillin, and mezuzot has to be done by hand with very stylized letter forms. If you look at a Torah scroll, you will see that the Hebrew letters differ from what you see in a book. This special alphabet is called *STaM*, an acronym for *sefarim, tefillin, mezuzot* ("[Torah] scrolls, tefillin, mezuzahs"), the three things that are written with it. The calligrapher who writes who uses this alphabet is called a *sofer* (scribe). He is trained in calligraphy, in making the quills that are used for pens in this type of writing, and in making a special kosher ink used for this purpose.

Scribes are trained by other scribes. The majority of them are Orthodox men. The Reform movement has a program to train Jewish calligraphers in the art of Torah writing so that they may become Reform scribes. Most scribes in America use an Ashkenazi (European) alphabet. There are also Torah scrolls that use a Sephardi (Spanish) alphabet. A trained scribe can look at the Torah scrolls in your synagogue and tell you where they came from and how old they are—just by the style of writing!

In addition to the special alphabet used for religious items, there are a many other decorative Hebrew alphabets. There is also a special writing called Rashi script, derived from a medieval form of Hebrew writing, which is now used much the way italics are used in English. There is an alphabet called Yerushalmi, based on Hebrew stone-cuttings found in Israel. Many calligraphers create their own designs.

Songs of Praise

Though not traditionally considered hiddur mitzvah, music provides another way to enhance a mitzvah. Examples of this are also found in the Bible. When the children of Israel crossed the Sea of Reeds, the prophetess Miriam used music to show her thanks to God: "Then Miriam the prophetess, Aaron's sister, took a timbrel in her hand, and all the women went out after her in dance with timbrels" (Exodus 15:20). King David was well known for playing the harp. The book of Psalms is actually a book of songs. Many of the psalms have introductory explanations, telling you what instruments are to accompany the singing of the psalm.

Throughout Jewish history, musical expression has been important religiously and culturally. The role of the hazzan (cantor) has developed as a musical enhancement of prayers. Jewish composers have often written synagogue music. It is possible to listen to synagogue music written by Salomon de'Rossi in sixteenth-century Italy, to purchase albums of Jewish music from medieval Spain and Europe, and to attend services with compositions by the nineteenth-century composers Louis Lewandowski or Salomon Sulzer, a Kiddush by the twentieth-century composer Kurt Weill, or a Kaddish by another twentieth-century composer, Leonard Bernstein. New compositions are being created by composers like Debbie Freedman. The music for the songs you sing at a service might be a very old traditional tune, a modern Hebrew composition, such as "Oseh Shalom" by Nurit Hirsch, or a song created by a modern American composer.

There is so much music that the Conservative and Reform movements put out songbooks related to the service. There are Jewish chorales in major cities that research and record music that was "lost." They also commission new compositions. There are individual composers creating music with Jewish themes. Their works are readily available in Jewish gift shops, and they tour the country performing in synagogues, Jewish community centers, camps, and concert halls.

עוֹשֶׂה שָׁלוֹם

שְׁמַע יִשְׂרָאֵל

אֲדוֹן עוֹלָם

כְּלֵי זֶמֶר

musical instruments

Itzhak Perlman, the Israel Philharmonic's solo violinist, is one of the world's most famous musicians. Perlman also specializes in klezmer music.

Some of the musical topics may be religious, such as a new version of Shema Yisrael or Adon Olam. Other musical topics explore cultural issues: becoming a Bar or Bat Mitzvah, oppression. Jewish music today reflects the variety that exists in the Jewish world. It is influenced by other forms of music, both Jewish and secular. In other words, there is something for everybody. Through this music it is always possible to fulfill the words of Psalm 98: "Sing to Adonai a new song."

Play It Again

As with the revival of traditional Jewish art, there has also been a revival of Jewish music. Klezmer, a form of Jewish music that was practically lost, has been rediscovered in our own time. Klezmer is a Yiddish word that comes from the Hebrew words *klay zemer,* "musical instruments." Klezmer was the Jewish folk music of Eastern Europe. It was played at weddings and other joyous occasions in the nineteenth and early twentieth centuries. Klezmer musicians played violin, clarinet, and other easily transportable instruments. They would travel from place to place playing their "gigs."

Around the country, musicians have rediscovered klezmer. Sometimes they get their material from old recordings. Some have researched musicians' notes, others have interviewed the last few surviving klezmer musicians. There are now klezmer groups throughout the United States. As might be expected, they reflect a number of styles. Some try to be pure, playing klezmer music the way it would have been heard in Russia or Poland over one hundred years ago. Others have discovered that klezmer blends well with newer musical styles and use instruments that did not exist in earlier decades. All these groups have breathed new life into an old art.

Teachings from Tradition

Then Moses and the Israelites sang this song to Adonai.

<Shemot 15:1>

Three things revive a person's spirit:
(happy) sounds, (beautiful) sights, and (glorious) scents.

<Shemot 15:20>

May the favor of Adonai our God be upon us, let the work of our hands prosper.

<Psalms 90:17>

Praise God with blasts of the horn, praise God with harp and lyre. Praise God with timbrel and dance, praise God with lute and pipe. Praise God with resounding cymbals, praise God with loud-clashing cymbals.

<Psalm 150: 3–5>

Praised is the One who created beauty in the world.

<Blessing upon seeing beautiful creatures and trees, based on Yerushalmi, Berachot 9>

Then Miriam the prophetess,	וַתִּקַּח מִרְיָם הַנְּבִיאָה
Aaron's sister,	אֲחוֹת אַהֲרֹן
took a timbrel in her hand,	אֶת־הַתֹּף בְּיָדָהּ
and all the women went out after her	וַתֵּצֶאןָ כָל־הַנָּשִׁים אַחֲרֶיהָ
with timbrels.	בְּתֻפִּים

<Berachot 57b>

JEWISH ORGANIZATIONS
Names, Addresses, Telephone Numbers, Fax Numbers, Internet Addresses, E-Mail

Yes! there is a Jewish Internet, and it's filled with up-to-the-minute events. The Internet is a terrific educational resource for all levels of students, and can add depth, interest, and commitment to your classroom discussions. All Jewish news outlets, magazines, and newspapers are on the Internet, so you can find the latest information on events relating to your classroom studies.

You can also conduct your own research by means of archives and libraries throughout the world. The Web is a worldwide network of computers, consisting of thousands of web sites. Most Jewish organizations have their own web sites, which detail the group's history, names, addresses, publications, and coming events. The following is a list of 100 Jewish social, political, religious, and educational organizations which can help you learn more about Jewish life in America and Israel—which can get them involved.

AGUDAH WOMEN OF AMERICA—N'SHEI AGU-
DATH ISRAEL
84 William St., Philadelphia, PA 19119 17200.
(215)247-9700. FAX: (215)247-9703.

AGUDATH ISRAEL OF AMERICA
84 William St.. NYC 10038. (212) 797-9000.

ALEPH: ALLIANCE FOR JEWISH RENEWAL 7318
Germantown Avenue, Philadelphia, PA 19119-1720.
(215) 247-9700. fax: (215) 247-9703.
e-mail: alephajr@aol.com; web: aeph.org

AMERICAN BOARD OF RABBIS-VAAD HARABAN-
IM OF AMERICA G.P.O.
Box 520, NYC 10016-0520.
(212) 714-3598. FAX: (800)539-4743.

AMERICAN JEWISH COMMITTEE
Institute of Human Relations, 165 E. 56th St., NYC 10022.
(212) 751-4000. FAX: (212)750-0326, web: www.ajc.org

AMERICAN JEWISH CONGRESS
Stephen Wise Congress House. 15 E. 84 St., NYC 10028.
(212)879-4500. FAX: (212) 249-3672.

AMERICAN JEWISH HISTORICAL SOCIETY
2 Thornton Rd., Waltham, MA 02154.
(617)891-8110. FAX: (617) 899-0208.
web: challenge.tiac.net/users/ajhs/index.html

AMERICAN JEWISH JOINT DISTRIBUTION
COMMITTEE—JDC
711 Third Ave., NYC 10017-4014.
(212)687-6200. FAX:(212)370-5467.
web: www.ort.org/communit/jdc/home.htm

AMERICAN JEWISH LEAGUE FOR ISRAEL
130 E. 59th St., NYC 10022.
(212)371-1583. FAX: (212)371-3265.

AMERICAN JEWISH PHILANTHROPIC FUND
122 E. 42nd St., 12 fl., NYC 10168-1289. (212) 755-5640.

AMERICAN JEWISH WORLD SERVICE
15 W. 26 St. 9th fl., NYC 10010.
(212) 683-1161. FAX: (212) 683-5187.

AMERICAN RED MAGEN DAVID FOR ISRAEL,
INC. [a.k.a. ARMDI & Red Magen David).
888 Seventh Ave., Suite 4030: NYC 10106.
(212) 757-1627. FAX: (212)757-4662.

AMERICAN SOCIETY FOR YAD VASHEM
48 W. 37 St., NYC 10018.
(212) 564-9606. FAX: (212)268-5002.

AMERICAN ZIONIST MOVEMENT
110 E. 59 St., NYC 10022.
(212)318-6100. FAX: (212)935-3578.
e-mail: info@azm.org, web: www.azm.org

AMERICAN ZIONIST YOUTH FOUNDATION, INC.
110 E. 59 St., NYC 10022.
(212)339-6002. (Israel Programs) or (212)339-6925.

AMIT WOMEN (formerly AMERICAN MIZRACHI
WOMEN) 817 Broadway, NYC 10003.
(212)477-4720.   web: www.ibm.net.il/amit

ANTI-DEFAMATION LEAGUE OF B'NAI B'RITH
823 United Nations Plaza, NYC 10017.
(212)490-2525. FAX: (212) 867-0779. web: www.adl.org

ASSOCIATION FOR JEWISH STUDIES
Brandeis University, MB 0001, LOWN 10, P
Box 9110, Waltham, MA 02254-9110.
(617)736-2981. FAX: (617)736-2982.

BAR-ILAN UNIVERSITY
http://www.biu.ac.il:80/BIU/

B'NAI B'RITH YOUTH ORGANIZATION
1640 Rhode Island Ave., NW, Washington, DC 20036.
(202)857-6633. FAX: (212)857-1099.

BEITAR JERUSALEM FOOTBALL CLUB
http://carmel.haifa.ac.il/~ssma599/beitar.html

B'NAI B'RITH WOMEN
L St., NW, Suite 250 Washington, DC 20036.
(202)857-1300. FAX: (202) 857-1380.

B'NAI B'RITH INTERNATIONAL
1640 Rhode Island Ave, N.W.
Washington D. C. 20036.
(202) 857 6600. http://bnaibrith.org

B'NEI AKIVA OF THE U.S. & CANADA
25 W. 26 St., NYC 10010.
(212) 889-5260. FAX: (212)213-3053.
e-mail: bneiakiva@israelmail.com, web: www.bneiakiva.org

BOYS TOWN JERUSALEM FOUNDATION OF AMERICA INC.
91 Fifth Ave., Suite 601, NYC 10003.
(212)242-1118. FAX: (212)242-2190.
e-mail: 74230.3450@compuserve.com,
web: www.boystownjerusalem.com

BRANDEIS-BARDIN INSTITUTE
1101 Peppertree Lane, Brandeis, CA 93064.
(805) 582-4450. (818) 348-7201, FAX: (805) 526-1398.
web: www.brandeis-bardin.org

CENTER FOR RUSSIAN JEWRY WITH STUDENT STRUGGLE FOR SOVIET JEWRY/ SSSJ
240 Cabrini Blvd., NYC 10033.
(212)928-7451.

CENTRAL CONFERENCE OF AMERICAN RABBIS
192 Lexington Ave., NYC 10016.
(212) 684-4990. FAX: (212)689-6419.
web: www.con.wesleyan.edu/~slinky/refjud.html

CHABAD'S CHILDREN OF CHERNOBYL
535 Fifth Avenue, New York, NY 10017.
(212) 681-7800.

CHABAD-LUBAVITCH
770 Eastern Parkway, Brooklyn, NY 11213.
(718) 493-9250
web: www.chabad.org

CLAL—NATIONAL JEWISH CENTER FOR LEARN-ING AND LEADERSHIP
99 Park Ave. NYC 10016-8012.
(212) 867-8888. FAX: (212) 867-8853.

COALITION FOR THE ADVANCEMENT OF JEW-ISH EDUCATION (CAJE)
261 W. 35 St., #12A. NYC 10001.
(212) 268-4210. FAX: (212)268-4214.
e-mail: 500-8447@mcimail.com

CONFERENCE OF PRESIDENTS OF MAJOR AMERICAN JEWISH ORGANIZATIONS
110 E. 59 St., NYC 10022.
(212)318-6111, FAX: (212) 644-4135.

DOROT
171 West 85th St., New York, NY 10024
(212) 769-2850.

EMUNAH WOMEN OF AMERICA
(formerly HAPOEL HAMIZRACHI WOMEN'S ORGANIZATION)
7 Penn Plaza, NYC 1000.
(212) 564-9045. (800)368-6440. FAX: (212) 643-9731.

EXECUTIVE UNION OF JEWISH
CONGREGATIONS OF AMERICA
333 Seventh Ave., NYC 10001.
(212) 563-4000. FAX: (212) 564-9058.

GRATZ COLLEGE
Old York Rd. and Melrose Ave. Melrose Park, PA 19027.
(215)635-7300, FAX: (215)635-7320.

HABONIM-DROR NORTH AMERICA
27 W. 20 St., 9th fl., NYC 10011.
(212) 255-1796. FAX: (212) 929-3459.

HADASSAH, THE WOMEN'S ZIONIST
ORGANIZATION OF AMERICA, INC.
50 W. 58th St., NYC 10019.
(212)355-7900. FAX: (212)383-8282.
web: www.hadassah.org

HEBREW COLLEGE
43 Hawes St., Brookline. MA 02146.
(617)232-8710, FAX: (617)734-9769. web: shamash.org/hc

HEBREW SEMINARY OF THE DEAF
4435 Oakton, Skokie, IL 60076.
(708) 677-3330. FAX: (708) 674-0327.

HEBREW UNION COLLEGE–JEWISH INSTITUTE
OF RELIGION
3101 Clifton Ave., Cincinnati, OH 45220.
(513) 221-2810.

HEBREW UNIVERSITY
http://www1.huji.ac.il/

HIAS, INC. (HEBREW IMMIGRANT AID SOCIETY)
313 Seventh Ave, NYC 1000 5004.
(212)967-4100. FAX: (212)967-4442.

HILLEL
1640 Rhode Island Ave. NW, Washington, DC 20036
(202) 857-6576. FAX (202) 857-6693.
web: shamash.nysernet.org/hillel

INSTITUTE FOR COMPUTERS IN JEWISH LIFE
7074 N. Western Ave., Chicago, IL 60645.
(312)262-9200. FAX: (312)262-9298.
ISRAEL HISTADRUT FOUNDATION
276 Fifth Ave., Suite 901, NYC 10003.
(212) 683-5454. (800) 443-4256. FAX: (212) 213-9233.

ISRAELI ALIYAH PROGRAMS CENTER
110 E. 59 St., 3rd fl., NYC 10022.
(212)339-6060. FAX: (212) 832-2594.

ISRAELI CITIES
http://www.ladpc.gov.il/citind.htm

ISRAELI EMBASSY, WASHINGTON, DC
http://www.israelemb.org/

ISRAELI MINISTRY OF TOURISM
htp://www.infotuor.co.il/

ISRAELI POP CHART
http://www.ctrl-c.liu.se/~dreamlover/anders/chart/israel/israel.html

JRUSALEM POST
http://www.jpost.co.il/index.html

JERUSALEM REPORT
http://www.jreport.virtual.co.il

JEWISH DAILY FORWARD
45 E. 33rd Street
New York, NY 10016
(212) 889-8200. FAX: (212) 447-6406.
web site: www.forward.com

JEWISH FAMILY SERVICES
5750 Park Heights Avenue Baltimor, MD 21215.
(410) 466-9200.

JEWISH GUILD FOR THE BLIND
15 W. 65 St. NYC 10023.
(212) 769-6240.

JEWISH MUSEUM
1109 Fifth Avenue, New York, NY 10128
(212) 423-3200.

JEWISH NATIONAL FUND OF AMERICA.
42 E. 69th St., NYC 10021.
(212)879-9300. FAX: (212)517-3293.

JEWISH RECONSTRUCTIONIST FEDERATION
1299 Church Rd., Wyncote, PA 19095.
(215)887-1988, FAX: (215)887-5348 web: shamash.org/jrf

JEWISH THEOLOGICAL SEMINARY OF AMERICA
3080 Broadway, NYC 10027-4649.
(212)678-8000. FAX: (212) 678-8947. web: www.jtsa.edu

JEWISH WAR VETERANS OF THE UNITED STATES
OF AMERICA 1811 R St., NW, Washington, DC 20009.
(202)265-6280, FAX: (202)234-5662.
e-mail: jwv@erols.com www.penfed.org\jwv\home.htm

JEWISH YOUTH INFORMATION LEAGUE
http://www.intac.com/~manning/jewishyouth/

JUDAH L. MAGNES MUSEUM
2911 Russell Street, Berkeley, CA.
(510) 549-6950. http://www.jfed.org/Magnes/Magnes.htm

KEREN OR, INC.
350 Seventh Ave., Suite 200, NYC 10001-5103.
(212)279-4070. FAX: (212)279-4043.

KFAR CHABAD, ISRAEL
972-3-960-7588.

KULANU, INC. (formerly AMISHAV USA)
1211 Ballard St., Silver Spring, MD 20910.
(301) 681-5679. FAX: (301) 681-5679.

LIKUD PARTY
http://usa.likud.org.il/index.html

MAZON: A JEWISH RESPONSE TO HUNGER 2940
Westwood Blvd, Suite 7. Los Angeles, CA 90064.
(310) 470-7769, FAX: (310)470-0736.

MERKOS L'INYONEI CHH. INC. (THE CENTRAL
ORGANIZATION FOR JEWISH EDUCATION)
770 Eastern Pkwy., Brooklyn. NY 11213.
(718)493-9250.

MILITARY
ftp://ftp.sunet.se/pub/picture/history/Israel/military/

NATIONAL COUNCIL OF JEWISH WOMEN
53 W 23 St. NYC 10010.   (212)645-4048.

NATIONAL COUNCIL OF YOUNG ISRAEL
3 W. 16th St., NYC 10011.
(212) 929-1525.

NATIONAL JEWISH COMMITTEE ON SCOUTING
(Boy Scouts of America)
1325 West Walnut Hill Lane. PO Box 152079, Irving, TX
75015-2079. (972)580-2119. FAX: (972) 580-7870
web: shamash.nysernet.org/scouts

NATIONAL JEWISH GIRL SCOUT COMMITTEE
Synagogue Council of America,
327 Lexington Ave.. NYC 10016.
(212)686-8670. FAX: (212(686-8673.

ORT, INC. ORGANIZATION FOR
REHABILITATION THROUGH TRAINING
817 Broadway, NYC 10030.
(212)353-5888. FAX:(212)353-5800.
gopher://ortnet.org:70/11/About%20ORT

PHILIP AND SARAH BELZ SCHOOL OF
JEWISH MUSIC
560 W. 185th St. NYC 10033-3201
(212) 960-5353.

POALE AGUDATH ISRAEL OF AMERICA, INC.
4405 13th Ave., Brooklyn, NY 11219.
(718)435-8228.

PROGRESSIVE ZIONIST CAUCUS
27 W. 20 St., NYC 10001.
(212)675-1168. FAX: (212) 929-3459.
E-mail: PZC@panix.com.

RABBINICAL COUNCIL OF AMERICA, INC.
305 Seventh Ave., NYC 10001.

RE'UTH WOMEN'S SOCIAL SERVICE, INC.
130 E 59 #51 NYC 10022.
(212)826-1570. (212)836-1114.

RECONSTRUCTIONIST RABBINICAL COLLEGE
Church Rd. and Greenwood Ave. Wyncote, PA 19095
(215)576-0800. FAX: (215) 576-6143
web: www.expresso.com/rrc/catalog2.htm

RELIGIOUS ZIONISTS OF AMERICA.
25 W. 26 St., NYC 10010.
(212)689-1414.

SHOMREI ADAMAH/KEEPERS OF THE EARTH
5500 Wissahickori Ave., #804C, Philadelphia. PA 19144.
(215)844-8150. FAX: (215)844-8243.

SIMON WIESENTHAL CENTER
9760 W.Pico Blvd., Los Angeles, CA 90035-4701.
(310)553-9036. FAX: (310) 553-8007.

SOCIETY FOR HUMANISTIC JUDAISM
28611 W. Twelve Mile Rd., Farmington Hills. Ml 48334.
(810)478-7610, FAX: (810)477-9014.

STATE OF ISRAEL BONDS
575 Lexington Ave., #60, NYC 10022.
(212)644-2663. FAX: (212)644-3925.

THE WORKMEN'S CIRCLE / ARBEITER RING

45 E 33rd St. NYC 10016.
(212) 889-6800. FAX: (212)532-7518.
TEL AVIV UNIVERSITY
http://www.tau.ac.il/

UNION FOR TRADITIONAL JUDAISM
241 Cedar Lane. Teaneck, NJ 07666.
(201)8010707. FAX: (201)801-0449.
web: www.utj.org/home

UNION OF AMERICAN HEBREW CONGREGATIONS

838 Fifth Ave., NYC 10021-7064.
(212) 249-0100. FAX: (212) 734-2857.
web: shamash.org/reform/uahc/index.html

UNITED JEWISH APPEAL, INC.
99 Park Ave., Suite 300, NYC 10016.
(212) 818-9100. FAX: (212) 818-9509.

UNITED STATES HOLOCAUST MEMORIAL MUSEUM

100 Raoul Wallenberg Place, SW, Washington, DC 20024.
(202)488-0400. FAX: (202)499-2690. web: www.ushmm.org

UNITED SYNAGOGUE OF
CONSERVATIVE JUDAISM
155 Fifth Ave., NYC 10010-6802.
(212)533-7800. FAX: (212)353-9439.

UNIVERSITY OF JUDAISM
15600 Mulholland Dr., Los Angeles, CA 90077.
(310)476-9777 FAX: (3I0)471-1278.

WOMEN'S AMERICAN ORT
315 Park Ave. S., NYC 10010
(212)505-7700. FAX: (212)674-3057.

WORLD JEWISH CONGRESS
501 Madison Ave.. 17th fl., NYC 10022.
(212)755-5770. FAX: (212)755-5883.

WORLD ZIONIST ORGANIZATION
gopher://shamash.nysernet.org/hh/wzo

YIVO INSTITUTE FOR JEWISH RESEARCH
555 W. 57 St., Suite 1100, NYC 10019.
(212)535-6700. FAX: (212)734-1062
web: www.ort.org/communit/yivo/start.htm

YOUNG JUDAEA
50 W. 58 St., NYC 10019.
(212)303-4575 FAX:(212)303-4572
web: www.hadassah.org

YOUTH DIVISION AND NORTH AMERICAN
FEDERATION OF TEMPLE YOUTH
PO Box 443, Bowen Rd., Warwick, NY 10990.
(914)987-6300 FAX:(914)986-7185.

ZIONIST ORGANIZATION
OF AMERICA
ZOA House 4 E. 34 St., NYC 10016.
(212)481 1500 FAX: (212)481-1515.

Index

Huleh Valley, 85
Humane slaughter, 92

I
Illness, 67
Immigrants, 41, 49-50
Inquisition, 19, 35, 70
Intermarriage, 108-109
Interpreters and translators, 19
Israel, love for, 39-41
Israel, State of, 19, 21, 22, 36, 62
    Children of Chernobyl, 68
    hesed shel emet in wartime, 77
    tourism, 43, 84-85, 109
Israel ben Joseph al-Nakawa, 13

J
Jacob ben Machir, 32
Jay Feinberg Foundation, 28
Jericho, 53
Jerusalem, 39, 40, 41, 42
Jerusalem Post, 113
Jerusalem Report, 113
Jewish Agency, 42
Jewish Alcoholics, Chemically Dependent Persons and Significant
  Others (JACS), 107
Jewish Community Relations Council (Chicago), 42
Jewish Daily Forward, 112
Jewish Family Services, 64, 106, 107, 109
Jewish Guild for the Blind, 28
Jewish National Fund (JNF), 42, 61, 84, 85, 87
Jewish Renewal, 93
Jewish Telegraphic Agency, 112, 113
Jewish Theological Seminary,

15, 41, 101
Jewish Vocational Services (JVS), 50, 64
Jewish War Veterans, 85
Jezreel Valley, 85
Joint Distribution Committee, 29, 35-37, 50, 51, 56, 57
Jokes, 114
Jones, Henry, 20
Judah Loew ben Bezalel, 76

K
Kaddish (mourner's prayer), 79, 123
Kantor, Mickey, 19
Keren Or, 29
Ketubah (marriage contract), 105, 108, 120, 122
Kiddush, 123
Kiddush cup, 120, 121
Kippah, 120
Kiruv, 109
Kissinger, Henry, 19
Kitzur Shulchan Aruch, 94
Klezmer, 124
Kohanim, 78
Kol yisrael arevim zeh la-zeh (all Jews are responsible for one
  another), 18, 20
Kristallnacht, 21

L
Labor Party, 43
Landsmanshaften, 49
Lasker Colony, 47
Legacy Fund Program, 39
Lender, Murray, 14
Leshon ha-ra (evil tongue), 113-114, 116
Levi ben Gershon, 32
Levites, 78
Lewandowski, Louis, 123

Liberty Bell, 38
Lifeline for the Old, 62
Likud Party, 43
Lilith, 113
Livnot U'Lehibanot, 39
Lower East Side, 17, 112
Lubavitcher Hasidism (Habad), 68, 76

M
Maccabee Forest, 83
Magellan, Ferdinand, 32
Magen David Adom, 27
Maimonides, Moses (Rambam), 8
    gleaning, 55
    kindness to animals, 95
    ladder of mitzvot, 55
    levels of tzedakah, 13, 14, 15
    marital advice, 105
    Mishneh Torah, 8
    physicians' oath, 25
    tomb, 40
Maot hittim (wheat money), 55, 56
Map-making and navigation, 17, 31, 32
Marriage counseling, 105
Matanot la'evyonim (gifts to the poor), 56
Mazon, 56, 57
Meditation, 93
Meir of Rothenburg, 34
Mentoring, 64
MERCAZ, 43
Mezuzah, 120, 121
Micah Publications, 93
Michael Reese Hospital, 25
Michelangelo, 118
Midstream, 113
Miriam, 123
Mi Sheberach (prayer for sick person), 72

PHOTO CREDITS

While every effort has been made to trace and acknowledge all the photos, we would like to apologize for any omissions.

AMERICAN JEWISH COMMITTEE; AMERICAN JEWISH CONGRESS; AMERICAN JEWISH HISTORICAL SOCIETY; ANTI-DEFAMATION LEAGUE; BNAI BRITH; BOY'S TOWN, JERUSALEM; CHABAD LUBAVITCH; DOROT; HADASSAH; JEWISH GUILD FOR THE BLIND; JEWISH NATIONAL FUND OF AMERICA; ORT; WORLD JEWISH CONGRESS.